PRAISE FOR THE AMERICAN BOOMERANG

It's the locker room at half time and the home team is listless, confused, and playing lousy. But Nick Adams has a powerful pep talk for Team USA that is just the kind of bracing, snap-out-of-it, kick-in-the-pants that a great nation needs to get back in the game to win. The American Boomerang *is more than a sorely needed love letter from Down Under—it's a timely, wise, and heartfelt plea to America to embrace its inherent exceptionalism.*

—Jack Fowler, publisher of National Review

The American Boomerang *should be compulsory reading for every American. It is a call to action, and an outside voice reminding us of our promise in the world. It reasserts the American virtues we have recently begun to abandon, like faith and freedom. Adams' conservative insight is invaluable and irresistible.*

—Ben Shapiro, Editor-at-Large, Breitbart.com

Foreigners, starting with Alexis de Tocqueville, have shown a unique understanding of the United States and what it means to be an American. Now Nick Adams, a young Australian, writes in this tradition, of old-fashioned American patriotism and courage—which aren't actually old-fashioned at all.

—Michael Barone, Washington Examiner

THE *American* boomerang

HOW THE WORLD'S GREATEST 'TURNAROUND' NATION WILL DO IT AGAIN

NICK *Adams*

FOREWORD BY LT. COL. ALLEN WEST

THE AMERICAN BOOMERANG

Published by WND Books®, Washington, D.C. WND Books is a registered trademark of WorldNetDaily.com, Inc. ("WND")

Book designed by Mark Karis

WND Books are distributed to the trade by:
Midpoint Trade Books, 27 West 20th Street, Suite 1102, New York, New York 10011

WND Books are available at special discounts for bulk purchases. WND Books, Inc., also publishes books in electronic formats. For more information, call (541) 474-1776 or visit www.wndbooks.com.

Unless otherwise indicated, Scripture quotations are taken from the Holy Bible, New International Version®, NIV®. Copyright © 1973, 1978, 1984, 2011 by Biblica, Inc.™ Used by permission of Zondervan. All rights reserved worldwide.www.zondervan.com.

First Edition
Hardcover ISBN: 978-1-936488-84-1
eBook ISBN: 978-1-936488-85-8

Library of Congress Cataloging-in-Publication Data
Adams, Nick, 1984-
The American boomerang : making the case for exceptionalism / Nick Adams ; foreword by Lieutenant Colonel Allan West.
pages cm
Originally published: Texas : Nick Adams, 2013.
ISBN 978-1-936488-84-1 (hardcover) -- ISBN 978-1-936488-85-8 (e-book)
1. Exceptionalism--United States. 2. National characteristics, American. 3. Civilization--United States. I. Title.
E169.1.A13 2014
973--dc23
2014012372
Printed in the United States of America
14 15 16 17 18 19 MV 9 8 7 6 5 4 3 2 1

For my mom and dad, who have always supported me.
I love you so very much.

CONTENTS

The cause of America is in a great measure the cause of all mankind. Many circumstances have, and will arise, which are not local, but universal, and through which the principles of all lovers of mankind are affected, and in the event of which, their affections are interested.

—Thomas Paine, 1776

I t was George Santayana who once quipped, "those who fail to learn from history are doomed to repeat it." That quote is normally used to refer to the recurrence of negative lessons that history teaches. However, this foreword is dedicated to a positive lesson that history is teaching America.

In 1831 a young Frenchman, Alexis de Tocqueville, was sent to America by the French government to study the American prison system. What resulted were two volumes of works released in 1835 and 1840 entitled, *Democracy in America*. The original mandate for which Tocqueville was dispatched did not garner his attention. What did attract this young man was the manner of the American society and its burgeoning sense of equality, not so much of outcomes but of opportunity.

Tocqueville stated, "Americans are so enamored of equality, they would rather be equal in slavery than unequal in freedom." It was that sense of individual freedom that was most interesting to him—and perplexing.

This young man found the good in America in the way

its societal organisms were ordered. Tocqueville realized the importance that faith played in weaving together the fabric that is America, "Liberty cannot be established without morality, nor morality without faith."

He came to realize what the grand experiment in liberty, freedom, and democracy recently launched by our Founding Fathers meant not just to Americans but to the world. He wrote, "America is great because she is good. If America ceases to be good, America will cease to be great."

But what exactly was it that made America great? What did it mean for America to be good?

It seems that this young Frenchman was prescient in his understanding of two very conflicting philosophies of governance. When Tocqueville expressed, "Democracy extends the sphere of individual freedom, socialism restricts it. Democracy attaches all possible value to each man; socialism makes each man a mere agent, a mere number. Democracy and socialism have nothing in common but one word: equality. But notice the difference: while democracy seeks equality in liberty, socialism seeks equality in restraint and servitude."

And so it is, the seminal confrontation that was identified some 180 years ago by a foreign traveler has returned. History has indeed repeated itself, but this time there is a positive lesson.

Today, instead of a young Frenchman, a young Australian has trekked across America to reawaken America to its greatness, its goodness, its exceptionalism.

His name is Nick Adams, and his book is appropriately entitled, *The American Boomerang*. And it is such an appropriate title because Nick takes the time to remind us of our foundational principles and values, and why America is important for the world. For Nick, it is time for the boomerang to return to its origin.

He writes, "The American possesses a distinctly bold boomerang nature. Carrying the characteristics of the Australia flying tool, he often embarks on a trajectory that travels him far from his origin, but always returns him to his founding position. Both the boomerang and the American are pioneer tools of self-determination, uniquely crafted in varying materials and size with an adventurous character, and free will."

Just as the words of Tocqueville reign supreme to this day, "The American Republic will endure until the day Congress discovers that it can bribe the public with the public's money." So shall the words of young Nick Adams find immortality for ages to come. When Nick defines American exceptionalism he uses a foresight and keen sense that every American should embody.

Nick says, "American exceptionalism is simple. It's individualism, not collectivism. Patriotism, not relativism. Optimism, not pessimism. Limited government, not welfare nanny-state. God, not government. Faith, not secularism, Life, not death. Equality of opportunity, not equality of outcome."

Just as Tocqueville realized the seminal confrontation between democracy and socialism, so does Nick Adams see the battle between conservatism and liberal progressive socialism.

Nick's book is a clarion call for America to arise, remember its goodness and greatness, and restore this Republic, not just for its own sake but for that of the world. To once again be that beacon of liberty. And as Tocqueville stated, "everybody feels the evil, but no one has courage or energy enough to seek the cure," Nick Adams' book *The American Boomerang* is all about the cure.

In sixteen concise chapters a young Aussie from "Down Under" so expressly captures the essence of what it means to hold the title of "American." He plainly lays out our DNA, our genetic code, and acutely identifies that which threatens the American genome. The legacy of America has always been the sincere desire to pass on better to subsequent generations than what was given unto ones own. At this time that promise of the American dream is in danger.

Tocqueville gave us two very insightful thoughts that echo to today: "Society is endangered not by the great profligacy of a few, but by the laxity of morals amongst all." And, "There are many men of principle in both parties in America, but there is no party of principle."

Nick Adams is the Alexis de Tocqueville of our times. He has written the twenty-first-century *Democracy in America*. He is admonishing us to restore our sense of high moral character and courage so as we not fall to the insidious, and dangerous, whims of the few. Nick is calling out for men and women of principle to stand guard for America in absence of political parties.

Nick Adams is simply asking us all to be an American Boomerang and return to our principled origins.

—*Allen B. West, Lieutenant Colonel, United States Army (Retired)*
Conservative Republican Member of the 112th Congress

T here is a war on America.

Never before has America come under such sustained attack from enemies, both foreign and domestic.

Most in the West rail against America and its culture. Proponents of Islam declare it the greatest evil. But there's more.

Anti-Americanism from outside would not be such a problem if Americans were united in standing up for their homeland. But this isn't the case. A growing number of Americans are against their *own nation*, believing it is getting what it deserves. And many don't realize they still live in the greatest country in the world, despite its clear failings and faults.

America is not always right, but it's the best thing we have. A strong and self-confident America is the best threat to the ascendancy of evil, and the greatest weapon against the values associated with the Western welfare state, secularism, and the modern-day Democratic Party. It is deeply concerning that America is behaving more and more as a retreating or reluctant superpower. There is no reason it should feel sheepish about its power, or seek to diminish its influence in the world.

Adversity is not new to America. Throughout its existence it has faced challenges. From the War of Independence to the Civil War to the Great Depression to the threat of the Russian Bear—in the end, America always prevailed.

In the fifteen years between 1930 and 1945, America came through the mass unemployment and hardship of the Great Depression to be victorious in World War II. The challenge of the Space Race in the twenty-five years after the war saw America hoist its flag on the moon. For the next twenty years, America acted as the catalyst for the collapse of communism and the U.S.S.R., leaving it the undisputed world superpower.

To this day, America still has the strongest economy, the best technology and its combined energy resources are the largest on earth. Decline is a choice, not a condition. I believe an American comeback is inevitable. But what remains to be seen is if such a return will resemble a bouncing ball, where America will never again reach its former height. Or will the comeback be boomerang-like, with America returning directly to its previous position?

These are matters that should concern all of us.

Anti-Americanism frustrates me. The decline of America terrifies me. That's why I am standing up to fight them both. This book should be a sharp incision in the heart of the Left's agenda.

With some external guidance, together we can achieve the boomerang effect, and bend the arc of history.

I developed a heart for America early. For as long as I can remember, all I ever wanted to do was visit.

As the afternoon sun would shine through my high school classroom in the suburbs of Sydney, I would often catch myself gazing out the window, dreaming about America. It didn't matter that by the age of sixteen I had already traveled to Europe half a dozen times and was the envy of my friends for it. All I wanted to do was get to America.

In fact, I distinctly remember one cold, late afternoon in January, standing on the Westminster Bridge in London with my parents. I was fifteen. Our London leg was the final stop in an extensive multi-country, multicity European tour. It had taken us from the mountains of Southern Germany to the breathtaking cities of Venice, Florence, and Rome, to majestic Paris, and to the lakes of Switzerland. I had seen everything from the Leaning Tower of Pisa to the Eiffel Tower to Buckingham Palace.

As we stood on the bridge overlooking the magnificent Palace of Westminster, home to the British Houses of Parliament, my father asked me if I had enjoyed the trip. I said, "Yes, but I really want to go to America." I will never forget my father's crestfallen face. How ungrateful I was!

But I couldn't help it. I was captive to its freedom. Excited by its flair. Attracted by its opportunity. Inspired by its story. Captured by its hope.

When I travel to America now, speaking to groups across the country, I'm often asked, "What do you love about America?" And for a long time, a pithy answer was not possible. Until one day, it dawned on me.

I love America because it is confident, competitive, courageous, faithful, idealistic, innovative, inspirational, charitable, and optimistic. It is everything as a nation that I wish to be as a person.

And then there's the other question I get: "What makes America exceptional?"

I'll tell you; American exceptionalism is simple.

It's individualism, not collectivism. Patriotism, not relativism. Optimism, not pessimism. Limited government, not nanny state. God, not government. Faith, not secularism. Life, not death. Equality of opportunity, not equality of outcome.

And America is special in that it is not just a country, geographical entity, or collection of fifty states; it's an idea.

This is why in five thousand years of recorded human history, we have never seen another country like America. It is indispensable to the world.

It's also why America elicits the most fevered emotions. An idea incites even more passion than a country. Ambivalence may be directed at the nation but seldom at the idea. This is why opinion on America ranges from misgivings to inspiration, misunderstanding to appreciation, loyalty to unfaithfulness, and approval to repudiation.

Ideas are distinct to nations; they develop almost instantly a common language of citizenship and infuse a national narrative with romance, fostering the virtues of patriotism and optimism. That's precisely what America has done. And the idea of America is, and will remain, deeply offensive to liberal or progressive agendas advocating collectivism, relativism, and greater government.

Conservative values, such as individualism, patriotism, Christianity, limited government, and support of Israel, are traditional American values. Sure, there exist paradox and inconsistency, but it cannot be said that the exceptions, no matter how stark, disprove the rule.

Think about it this way: If you compare the progressive ideological position with the foundational American position, on every count, they are poles apart. The Left believe in a collectivist society; the constitutional American in the individual. The Left subscribe to cultural relativism; the conservative American is the most patriotic of souls. The Left believe in more government and greater regulation; the freedom-loving American is antiauthority and deeply suspicious of government. The Left promotes radical multiculturalism; the American, *E pluribus unum*. The Left is uncomfortable with a world superpower and dislikes the concept of the nation-state; the patriotic American can't stomach the United Nations. The Left is the loudest in support of Palestine; the traditional American a great friend of Israel. The Left has reservations and seeks to intervene in markets; the informed American is the greatest and purest capitalist alive. See what I mean? The list goes on. Chalk and cheese.

For this reason, in the Leftist hierarchy of beliefs, anti-American autocracy is the trump card that beats gay rights, feminism, race, and freedom of speech (not that the Left ever really believed in that, anyway). When you throw in envy (of American achievement and power) to the mix, it is not surprising that anti-Americanism has become a sport among some. As the world superpower and a conservative idea in a globe of socialism, America will never be loved. But that does not matter. What matters is its continued success and strength. It is far better to be respected, even feared, than loved.

I wanted to write this book, not just in response to rampant anti-Americanism, but because it disturbed me that it was becoming common, for Americans and non-Americans alike, to celebrate American weakness, to revel in a sedated America, and to seek to deride and remove all the things that made America exceptional.

Four weeks before I first arrived in America, at the G20 summit in spring 2009, President Barack Obama was asked if he believed in American exceptionalism. I was shocked at his answer.

He said, "I believe in American exceptionalism, just as I suspect that the Brits believe in British exceptionalism and the Greeks believe in Greek exceptionalism."[1] Given their impact on me, I can only imagine how those words struck at the souls of tens of millions of proud Americans.

The domestic politics of America is an internal matter for Americans, but it is obvious that President Obama's administration is the first with clear and stated sympathies for a European-based secular-left model, a sharp departure from the America of founding and of recent times.

And the third question I'm always asked is: "Why does an Australian care about America?"

Now, that's a really easy one. What is good for America is good for the world. The world's fortunes travel with America. It is in the interests of every person to keep America strong. In fact, I consider it the great moral imperative of our time— because everything hangs on it.

I'll tell you what else I love about America. It embraces risk and entrepreneurs, and it is the country where you can be down-and-out over and over and over, but always come back. I love America because its cultural conservatism is profoundly at odds with liberal or progressive agendas. It is the cultural conservatism of the American that offends most. But it must be always remembered that without sound economic management and a stable economy, the attainment of cultural conservative ends is impossible.

The American belief in human freedom, accompanied by powerful personal and civic Christian faith, provides a robust individualism and notable libertarian streak. This unique synergy produces the most individualistic, optimistic, moralistic, patriotic, religious, and libertarian nation of the world. Its closest English-speaking cultural cousins, including even its fellow frontier nation and most steadfast ally, Australia, bear little resemblance.

But America being unlike anyone else is not a new phenomenon.

Alexis de Tocqueville was a French philosopher who visited America about 180 years ago. He was just twenty-six. For nine months, he traveled through the country. Five years later, he wrote about the greatness of America. Since then, there has been virtually no recorded foreign observation and analysis of American exceptionalism.

As far as I know, Tocqueville's book, *Democracy in America*, remains the only time in America's history that an outsider has written a comprehensive account of his or her journey through the land. It is a classic, and a must-read for every American who is interested in his or her own history.

The world was a starkly different place when Tocqueville penned his masterpiece, but his prescience and observations are almost frighteningly brilliant. To America's detriment, his reading of American life and culture, and his conclusions that various national characteristics made America exceptional, do not receive the attention they deserve. In a world gripped by cultural relativism, his opinions have little place.

Over a series of trips, I have spent nine months traveling the continental United States, the exact length of Tocqueville's famous journey. Crisscrossing the nation from west to east, north to south, visiting more than twenty states by plane, train, car, bus, and horse and cart, I observed the character and culture of a people who had captured my heart and imagination even as a young child. From small towns to big cities, deserts to forests, museums to rodeos, city lights to ranches, and suburban homes to businesses, I felt the excitement of the heady and steady pulse of American exceptionalism.

Clearly, I arrived in America with a substantial prejudice. I had a fascination for the nation that had blossomed from childhood, with the maturing of my Christian faith and time at university, I developed a staunchly pro-American perspective. And just as the deal was being sealed, along came September 11.

I remember, as a seventeen-year-old in September 2001, watching helplessly and hoping wordlessly by the television as the cowardly and positively evil acts of a team of freedom-haters were repeatedly replayed. I remember my mother rushing into my room. And I will forever hear the sobbing and wails of young and old the next day as they spontaneously gathered to watch the TV in a local shopping center.

I knew immediately that my politics and worldview had been forever changed. I knew then and there that it was my responsibility to embrace and defend the American nation. I understood that history had a capacity to bestow upon a generation a particular role and this was it.

It would not be honest of me to conceal my political convictions. I believe in God, the traditional family, personal responsibility, and the sanctity of human life; in patriotism, self-reliance, and individual liberty; in free markets and limited government; in the state of Israel and a strong national defense; and that welfare should be ideally the role of nongovernment actors, particularly the church and family.

Before arriving in the country, I was hardly aware that these very convictions were the engine of American exceptionalism, but now it makes sense that a love for America is in the DNA of every conservative.

The time for an analysis of American greatness could hardly be better. The end of American power and influence— and the inevitable ascent of China—has been declared. Not only do I thoroughly disagree with these conclusions, but I consider it essential, once more, for an outside voice to express the potential that this country has to offer human civilization.

Let it be clear—we are not operating in a post-American world. It still stands comfortably as the greatest country of the world. It still enjoys freedoms unlike those found anywhere else. The American dream is still the dream of millions across the globe. It's unique among the nations of the earth. But America is falling behind— not behind other nations, but behind her promise and potential.

It's a problem when America romances the economic and government ideas of Europe. It's concerning that American businesses and individuals are more encumbered by red tape than ever before. And it is utterly devastating that American classrooms are increasingly captive to the academic elite, with many schools active in removing all references to God and the Bible, and teachers prone to imparting their own jaundiced views on the Constitution and Declaration of Independence. Not to mention their encouragement of victimhood through politically correct social campaigns. The elites who hold such influence over America are increasingly separated from it.

As one close American friend suggested to me, "Sometimes it takes someone on the outside to tell us or remind us what we are like on the inside." And perhaps it is fitting that an Australian be the one to do it. As an Australian, I am proud that my nation has been America's most intimate and steady ally and the only nation to have fought alongside America in every major conflict since World War I.

My book is aimed at every American who believes in the foundational idea and values of America. It should remind the reader that despite the anti-Americanism lurking in the world and the negativity screamed on the front pages of newspapers, America is, for all her shortcomings, a fountainhead of everything we consider great or noble in mankind.

Some will suggest many of my analyses are naïve and romanticized. To them I say, I have fresh and unique eyes, and I accept the advantages and disadvantages that sight carries. More than anything, it is a personal testament intended for future generations.

In this book, I continually refer to "Americans." By that I mean patriotic, God-fearing Americans, each of whom represents the idealized American, but by no means *every* American. Culturally conservative with a providential worldview, these Americans are people of family, faith, flag, and neighborhood, defined by the belief that their past achievements, future opportunities, and blessings come from their Creator, not their government. Patriotic Americans are proudly principled, passionately individualistic, and resolutely self-determined, believing every person can rise above the circumstances of birth to achieve any outcome. This definition clearly excludes some. But it is my hope that I can help those Americans see and become such citizens. I also refer to "an outsider" or to other nations. Clearly, the "outsider" does not represent every person from a foreign country. I am a case in point.

The idealism of America is what makes it so great. To overcome its trials of today, it must once more embrace the ideas that inspired and motivated the Founders and that inspired me to pen this book.

Of the threats to America, none presents greater danger than a school of thought, either espoused by government or contemplated by ordinary Americans, that American exceptionalism does not exist.

American exceptionalism is not an opinion or moral judgment but a testable and provable hypothesis; more than that, it is a foundational cultural value of America. Any action or commentary that throws this into question, fundamentally changes America. There is a deeply-held belief that if America was not that powerful, and didn't proclaim its exceptionalism, people would like it more. As a result, there appears to be an emerging trend of American leadership to retreat, or "play nice." Both the assumption and consequent trend are extremely naive. Rather than buying international goodwill that exists mainly on paper only, it is received as weakness and emboldens competitors and adversaries alike. America needs to be more concerned with good outcomes, than good intentions.

In my view, the doctrine of relativism is as dangerous to Western civilization as radical Islam and communism. Anti-Americanism can be understood through the lens of relativism: if nothing is any better than anything else, then success is unjust. Our war is as much with the media and academic corridor that espouse this doctrine as it is with the perpetrators of September 11. Political correctness gives life to these great threats. By believing in everything, relativism believes in nothing. It asserts that no culture, religion, nation, or person is any more successful than or superior to any other. Perhaps the twenty-sixth president of the United States, Theodore Roosevelt, put it best: "The man who loves other countries as much as his own stands on a level with the man who loves other women as much as he loves his own wife."

It is culture that determines character. And it will be the winner of the kulturkampf that will determine the fate of the union. A great animating impulse of this nation has always been the view that it had a moral mission. It is the duty of all to assist America to meet that obligation, and the expectations associated with it.

I need to say thank you to all those who helped create, support, and complete this project. But the greatest thank-you must be directed first and foremost to the idea and nation of America, her military, and her people. America's leadership of the world and its undying friendship based on freedom and democracy have inspired generations. Without America, darkness would cover the world.

Liberty, justice, democracy, and bravery are the principles you have advocated and protected at enormous cost. I appreciate and applaud you.

God bless America.

—*Nick Adams, Highfield, Australia, July 2014*

The Cowboy Spirit

A nyone who visits this great land for the first time is immediately struck by her sheer size and scale. With fresh eyes overwhelmed by the impressive display of the busy cities, the open expanses of land, and the beauty of nature, a smile undoubtedly forms. And one thought: hope.

This must be how the first cowboys felt.

The first settlers of the Wild West, pioneers by necessity and visionaries by choice, struck out in wild and unknown territory to tame the land, make a living, raise a family, and build their own piece of heaven on earth.

Today, with all the technology and resources available to them, in reality, Americans aren't that far removed from those first cowboys. They may not wear boots, but they walk the same ground. They may not be as rugged, but they have the same tough spirit. They may not carry six-shooters, but they'll stand up for their freedom and defend what they hold most dear. No matter what race. No matter what background. No matter what generation.

If they are honest with themselves, there's a little John Wayne in all of them.

With a little effort, you can instinctively imagine the feelings of the earliest Americans upon first viewing the stunning vista of the unspoiled frontier, with all its arresting seduction. Overwhelmed. Excited. Maybe even a little scared and apprehensive. But ready. Americans have always liked a challenge.

While the contemporary American landscape may be eminently different from those first visions of a new land, it is still able to move, impose, and overpower the mind. This land has matchless variety, beauty, energy, and life. It is so diverse that visitors could be forgiven for thinking that the fifty states are fifty varying countries. And it doesn't matter in which geographical location of the country you may find yourself—be it the Iowan cornfields, the rolling farmland of Ohio, the prairies of Illinois, the riverbanks of Missouri, or the glaciers of Montana, the distinctive diversity of nature mirrors the unique properties of the landscape of the American culture. It's unmistakable. Irresistible. Exceptional.

With more than three hundred million people living in a continental landmass stretching over some three thousand miles, this country achieves the implausible: the fusing of diversity and uniformity, separating herself from all other nations. This leads to an inescapable conclusion: this nation and its people are profoundly different from any other. Always have been. Always will be.

To outsiders, the enormous paradox of patriotic Americans is that they are a people possessing equal doses of extreme individualism and unified nationalism—a blend unique to America. But the Founding Fathers were men intent on preserving the differences between this land and other nations for generations to come. They fled from an overbearing central government and state religion. They wanted a new identity. A new life. A dream they could pass down to their children, and the conviction that hard work did make a difference. You could thrive. You could *become* instead of merely exist.

Most modern-day Americans still praise their Founders today for the risks they took. Drafting their nation's first documents was not easy. Having to account for the needs of millions of people in a fair and agreeable manner was not easy. The wars fought to protect their freedoms were not easy. But as they say, nothing worth having comes easy.

The Founders were highly suspicious of government. They favored the citizen. They supported freedom. They wanted to maximize protection of citizens' rights. This is the reason primacy of freedom throughout America is no mere coincidence. *It isn't just something in the water.* Today, there is a growing number who still insist that the rights of every citizen be protected from an overly powerful central government. They are passionate about their sovereignty and zealous about their rights. They celebrate their ideals with volume and vibrancy, and they ground the culture and communities of this country. Fervor for these values still streaks through them.

They demand an active role in shaping the rules that govern their world, past merely voting for their officials. They insist that their officials listen. They expect to know that their concerns are acted upon. They refuse to be more than an election statistic. They demand to be seen as individuals who together create and celebrate their country's strength.

It's a small-town feel versus a big-government fiasco. *It's the difference between Mayberry and mayhem.*

***

From the gospel music, mint juleps, and sultry belles of the South, to the snowy wastes of Minnesota, to the spectacular canyons of Nevada, this land they call America is different from all other nations in important ways. Here each person is an individual, a character, an identity. The individualism of this land is its foundational difference. In the presence of this fierce individuality, all dullness flees, and man is once more animated, far away from the inertness of the foreign society. This nation can never be called a bore.

We can thank the early Calvinist settlers for this—men and women who believed in the importance of the individual and his or her direct relationship with God. Highly individualistic and untypical Europeans, these immigrants desperately sought the soil of economic opportunity. Self-reliance, independence, and exceptionalism, the themes of Calvinist thought that spread with great speed from the eastern frontier westward, quite clearly remain the defining attributes of the American experience today.

Americans have dodged the foreign bullets of the world, bullets that have put thousands of holes in the virtue of individualism. The concept is elegant in its simplicity. While individuality is the driver of innovation and creativity, group-think produces mediocrity and drudgery. Those living in an individualistic society are less likely to believe they are entitled automatically to a share of anything, are less troubled by inequality, and are driven to provide for themselves and their families through their own effort. Sounds fair and reasonable. *But to the Left, the concept of personal responsibility threatens their entire vision.* That's why the assault on America is permanent.

Patriotic Americans expect little and believe all to be possible. Influencing virtually every aspect of culture and central to the possibility and existence of the American dream, this attitude is, along with Christianity, the explanation of extraordinary American accomplishment. Americans believe that any individual can rise above the circumstances of birth and achieve anything he or she strives to achieve. There is no class of people forever condemned to poverty or guaranteed wealth. Patriotic Americans believe in equality of birth, not equality of result. They have a God, but it is not government.

There appears to be, with only the notable exception of those who describe themselves as liberal, hardly a citizen anywhere in America who views individual success as contingent on government or union support. Conventional, self-governing Americans are not likely to look on the state as either the provider of benefits or the guarantor of equal outcomes; Americans are far more concerned with doing what they must to make ends meet. They cannot conceal their contempt for and aversion to regulation or taxation.

***

The values of this nation that transform and transcend society serve as the bone and sinew of the American life. Among these are the virtue of optimism and the comfort of certainty.

One visit to this grand land reveals an instinctively culturally conservative and optimistic society, a stark contrast to the state of all other Western nations that are full of, according to Italian philosopher Marcello Pera, "agnosticism, of relativism, of disenchantment, of presumption."[1] Patriotic Americans are possibly the only people on this earth who do not wrestle with their identity; they know, without the slightest hint of doubt, who they are. And these are citizens for whom identity is a choice, not legacy.

Patriotic Americans hold their values dear; the values are robust and unyielding and only increasing in utility. This moral ecology separates patriotic Americans from their peers, perpetuating the idea of exceptionalism. They *are* different. And proud of it. Good on them.

A person of principle is extraordinary; so is a nation that is founded on principles. The traditions of a nation define its culture, and America's culture is one that does not demand conformity with set customs. Rather it is a culture that fosters the individual and his or her character, leaving any outsider convinced of the exceptional nature of the tradition of independence.

Individual freedom, political liberty, justice, republican democracy, and bravery are matters of the American heart. This heart ensures morality trumps even law—this is their Judeo-Christian legacy. They are principles that form the beat of its mighty pulse. These enduring founding principles have translated to lasting values. Powerful Christianity, muscular patriotism, and strength of the military are blended with the values found in the typical American household. Most impressively, Americans genuinely assert and believe that their values afford them moral and cultural superiority. They do. *America offers the greatest number of people the best chance at a free and prosperous life. Period.*

No matter the background or the culture, Americans are eloquent and forthright in explaining and defending their values. And they do, twenty-four hours a day, seven days a week. After all, there is little purpose in possessing enduring values unless they are celebrated and actively pursued. Americans get it. Being afraid to speak your values is as good as possessing none. And outspoken people of principle and value raise the ire of highly sensitized and meek populations. *Nothing yellow about Americans.* A strong national identity thwarts the efforts of international institutions to meddle in the American people's business, and that's an added bonus.

The simplistic and uncompromising convictions of patriotic Americans bring enormous discomfort in societies where personal freedoms are shamed from birth and where backing down or getting out of the way is seen as noble. Put a patriotic American in a room with another English-speaking person, hailing from a nation that extends similar liberties, but one where they aren't celebrated and revered, and the two might have a hard time discussing much past the weather, world events, fashion, or sports. They would speak the same language. Or would they really?

This creates both pride and controversy. An individual with values-emphasis is an automatic candidate for, and subject of, envy and loathing. A proud American's convictions can easily spark an anti-American disease. *American national character must be understood in the context of its creation—that of a self-made society.*

This reveals a world of difference to those within the conformist society who quietly participate and submit. In the world's eyes, the manner, style, and views of the American are perceived as unrestrained and irritable. The rare cowboy in those countries is seen as a nuisance to be exterminated in those countries. There, cowboys don't do the shooting; they're the ones who get shot. That cowboy spirit is neutered like the family pet. Americans lead; if international consensus is there, that's great. If it isn't, Americans aren't going to shed a single tear. They will bound right out into battle, alone. They don't do appeasement; just ask the Japanese. America is the alpha male in the world house. A good thing, too. Under the recent leadership, this hasn't been the case, and the world has suffered as a result. While international goodwill is an essential tool for global cohesion, America should never be falling over itself, in pursuit of its purchase. Never should it surrender anything in its control because anything you give away at the stroke of a pen, you only get back at the barrel of a gun.

Americans' innate insistence on the defense of freedom at any price is counterbalanced by the apathetic nonchalance of their Western cousins. In America, conformity is no virtue, nor is it fostered by culture. To favor silence, even in disagreement, which is a common trait in other cultures, is considered here the epitome of weakness. The domain of only the limp-wristed and lily-livered. In America, people are instructed from an early age to characterize submission that is unaccompanied by struggle as shameful. As it should be. Leaders, and not merely sheep, must be bred.

Though differing views and opinions may lead to disagreements, the resulting discussion can often lead to renewed confidence, strengthened relationships, and added character. And who doesn't love someone with character? You bet it counts.

***

Even today, America is full of cowboys and cowgirls; this rough and rugged spirit is one of the most recognizable American images in the world.

Where other cultures are quick to criticize the cowboy as old-fashioned, masculine, and anti-intellectual, America still embraces him warmly. In fact, it is difficult to consider the cowboy persona as anything other than the natural state of man. Unless you are hopelessly and frustratingly politically correct. And then you don't really count anyway.

Though the cowboy spirit may not be as alive and prevalent in America as it once was, it is far more alive and customary here than anywhere else in the world. This enduring personification of American society and her values does not ride in groups. The American "cowboy" and "cowgirl" have only their horses and bare necessities; they are people of action without assistance. It's why candidates for political office in America clamor for a photo on horseback, where in most other Western countries such a photograph would be considered "bad optics" for any aspiring politician. That horse is synonymous with freedom. Self-made, free, and self-reliant, the cowboy exudes confidence, certainty, and strength: the ultimate success. More refreshing than a cold drink on a hot day, the cowboy is exhilarating in the world of the meek, weak, and gray. The confidence of the American individual sets him apart from others. From the taste for risk to the belief in limited government, evidence of this confidence is everywhere. These are not fearful positions, and so it must be concluded that confidence is an American trait. For a country like America, and a people like the Americans, treading water is the same as drowning. The world needs America to be a country of self-reliant warriors, not government-dependent, politically correct pussycats. Leave that to Europe.

A strong national identity thwarts the efforts of international institutions to meddle in the American people's business, and that's virtuous.

Old Glory

To imagine a nation more defined by its borders, language, and culture than America is challenging. As a virtue chiseled in the bedrock of morality, loving one's nation is perhaps only second in rank to service to one's country. Americans have long been a nation full of citizens ready to pay the ultimate sacrifice for their country.

Few people could refute the steady and sustained attack on the virtue of patriotism since the conclusion of the last world war. And patriotism sure has gotten a bad rap over the years. It is today mostly considered by other countries as poor form, an outdated, anti-intellectual, prejudicial, bellicose, and even immoral state. What a crock.

Just ask the French how this stance worked out for them. Their experiment after the First World War of embracing internationalism and pacifism and painting the pages of their children's textbooks with the colors of surrender decimated their national will. *Merci*, teacher's union. It ate at their resolve. And their superior military meant nothing when the Nazis came for them. It was all over before you could say *bonjour*. They folded like a cheap suit.

Thankfully, while the rest of the world does internationalism, America does patriotism. American patriotism is as deep as it is wide. Today's adults have been shaped by the events of the twentieth century; older Americans explain that their patriotism and nationalism deepened greatly during the two world wars. Younger Americans remember exactly when and where they were when the Twin Towers fell. Different horrific events but the same outcome. And time and time again, the same symbol of freedom has captivated them and rallied them like no other—the American flag. Flown for victory on the battlefield. Waved with enthusiasm in parades and events. Carefully and lovingly folded in tearful remembrance for a loved one lost in the line of duty. Raised in defiance of terrorists. Glorious always.

Patriotism is social and cultural glue; it affects every facet of human nature. Outsiders must conclude that American patriotism is responsible for its citizens confidence and incentive to be the acme of the world. Patriotism affords unity, strength, inclusion, and dominance of the world in every field, its roots firmly planted in the transcendent values of individual freedom, Christianity, justice, and democracy. *No one* does patriotism like an American. It's inspiring. *And I'll tell you something else you won't hear in the mainstream media: America wins respect in the world when it displays who it is, not what self-appointed cultural dieticians want it to become. That's the truth.*

Americans consider each achievement of their country

a personal victory. But more than this, they appear entirely unselfish in remembering their nation at all times. They are prone to nostalgia. They recognize that history is to the nation what memory is to the individual. Any earnest conversation with an American reveals the American's clear understanding that no one can tell where he is today or where he will find himself tomorrow unless he knows where he has come from. Americans may currently think yesterday was better than today but hold tight to the truth that God never performs His greatest feats in our yesterdays.

***

A string of thirty-one words, the Pledge of Allegiance is perhaps the greatest example of American exceptionalism. Recited by citizens standing and facing the American flag, with their right hands over their hearts, it succinctly encapsulates the fervor and flavor of the American patriotic condition. Until the scourge of "political correctness" found its way into their lives, it was hard to find a man, woman, or child anywhere in this land unable to recite the words of the Pledge. Events and meetings were started with it, and schoolchildren recited it daily.

But still, the Pledge gets recited frequently. And it's the only one of its kind in the world. It is a most unforgettable experience to stand amid Americans of all stripes at the beginning of public events and meetings, witnessing firsthand the swift, automatic shuffle of feet and collective pivoting of bodies in the direction of the hanging American flag. For words recited so often, they could easily be recited automatically, free of emotion. Yet voices invariably ring with passion, and the earnest faces, fixed eyes, and stern concentration are commensurate with the gravity of the words. From a cacophony of voices comes a united chorus. Out of many, one. No other country in the world has an equivalent of this pledge to the values of liberty and justice, or of its frequent recitation. *Patriotism matters.*

***

"Old Glory" was a term first coined by patriot William Driver, a nineteenth-century sea captain. His beloved American flag was flown aboard his ship in 1831, and when he retired, he continued to fly it every chance he got. It was an outward expression of an inward pride in his country.

The visibility of a country's flag within its own borders should always be seen as a measure of greatness and strength. But the nation and its people who merely fly it from the government building miss the point. The simple action of a man flying his flag outside his home in other lands, even other Western countries, is considered different at best, obnoxious by most. This is a glaring contrast to the millions of homes and shops in thousands of towns that proudly display the American flag. They understand.

Patriotic Americans don't tolerate mistreatment of their flag. It's one flag that doesn't get messed with. They even have specific protocols regarding the use and care of the flag. Incomparable in detail, they exist for its folding, displaying, hanging, and carrying. Every occasion, location, and context is covered, ranging from the procession to the funeral, the car to the home, mourning to celebration, the podium to the window, and the location of the flag when present with other flags.

It should be no surprise that from the foothills of the Appalachians in North Carolina to Nevada, from Los Angeles to New York, and everywhere between, the love of the American flag is on view. As you crisscross small towns and big cities, irrespective of population or demography, you find flags adorning streets, shopping centers, office buildings, homes, graves, mailboxes, taxis, buses, cars, and gas stations. And these are not simply temporary decorations; they are permanent fixtures of patriotic pride. To Americans, they are daily reminders of their great country. To a visitor or an immigrant, they bring a strange sense of reassurance, comfort, and inclusion.

Favored by business, sports, and entrepreneurs, the national colors of red, white, and blue (often with accompanying stars and stripes) show up on logos, mascots, shop fronts, and products. And it's not uncommon for a citizen to bring a flag along while traveling to another country. Americans never forget their homeland, no matter where in the world they may find themselves.

While studying in China, a California student was staying in a university dorm. This young man approached his roommate, expressing a desire to hang up his American flag on the outside of their door. The approach was polite but firm and confident, and the roommate didn't have any opposition to a suggestion put so reasonably. In fact, he was amazed at the intense pride in this man's country that had inspired him to carry his flag halfway around the world, and at his eagerness to proclaim it in a foreign country.

While that may not sound like anything to write home about, American patriotism is often greatly admired from afar. The words of international English sports star David Beckham most certainly show Americans that they should fully appreciate and preserve what they have:

> I've been lucky to have been a pretty regular visitor to America since I was a boy. Time enough to get to know a country that I've grown to love . . .
>
> If I could take one aspect of American life back to England with me, it would be this country's sense of patriotism; the feeling of a whole nation united under one flag. Maybe the pride Americans take in their country is one of the reasons why sports stars here seem to enjoy a level of respect that's not always the case in Europe. Heroes of mine like Michael Jordan, Tiger Woods, Andre Agassi and Michael Johnson have been pushed on to greater achievement, I'd say, because they know they've got the unqualified support of the whole country behind them when they go into action.
>
> These sporting greats . . . have taken advantage of being born and raised in the land of opportunity. The American Dream is founded on the same principles as my own: if you work hard enough, there never needs to be a limit on how far life can take you.[1]

The American dream is fused with patriotism; the two are inseparable in these parts. A sporting event becomes a moving spectacle where athletes and crowds sing their national anthem with all the intensity and concentration they can muster, with moist eyes and the hand covering the heart.

It is hard not to admire the American man—a man unafraid to speak of, and expect, greatness. Overt displays of pride are mainstream and encouraged. But it must also be noted that man here is yet to be feminized to the same extent as in many other countries. The idealized American man is perceived as assertive and always fearless, valuing masculine traits and confident in his crusading ethos and patriotic proclamations. *Although, don't worry, the Left are hard at work to change this. They are doing their absolute best to bring about the wussification of America.* Emotion over national pride, even in the form of tears, is still seen as a deep strength and a devout love of country.

Critics of America conveniently ignore the ambition and success of the American project. Where recent history has shown the rest of the world seeking the divisions of nations into microstates to resolve matters of conflict, America hosts an incredibly large and diverse population, living under the one federal government, in peace.

***

There is said to be almost 3.8 million square miles of American soil, and there is not a stretch within the land without something bearing a name of historical or cultural connection. Streets, restaurants, buildings, businesses, towns, schools, hotels, and cities are named Liberty, Independence, Constitution, and Freedom. Americans even celebrate these values on their currency. Repetition is the mother of retention—patriotism is everywhere.

Embedded in the Great Seal of the United States of America, as well as on American money, is *E pluribus unum*, the Latin phrase for "Out of many, one." There is no phrase that better accounts for or reflects the exceptional mentality and society of the American citizen than this.

The American's fixed eye on national unity and its virtues are sharply focused, an eyesight inherited from the Founding Fathers. In the Federalist Papers, the first American Supreme Court chief justice, John Jay, noted in 1787:

> Providence has been pleased to give this one connected country to one united people—a people descended from the same ancestors, speaking the same language, professing the same religion, attached to the same principles of government, very similar in their manners and customs . . . This country and this people seem to have been made for each other, and it appears as if it was the design of Providence, that an inheritance so proper and convenient for a band of brethren, united to each other by the strongest ties, should never be split into a number of unsocial, jealous, and alien sovereignties.[2]

America is indeed the "melting pot" of nations, united in its diversity of cultures and skin, Immigrants here are expected to assimilate to mainstream society by surrendering their differences; a self-proclaimed hyphenated American is treated with suspicion and derision, and the visitor feels little sympathy. In this land, a hyphenated identity is most un-American. Allegiance to a nation other than one's home may be common for citizens of other nations, but the American recoils at the prospect. Don't like it here? Leave.

When immigrants are expected to submit to the dominant culture of their new home, cohesion, success, and the exceptional can flourish. Ideally, new immigrants and *Mayflower* descendants alike are glued together by the English language, a belief in the American dream, and the values of freedom, justice, and equality of birth but not outcome. That's American.

There are discernible dangers within range. An unconscionable number of men, women, and children cross the borders of this nation illegally every day. For all their strength, Americans appear uncharacteristically helpless in stopping such lawlessness. In many parts of this land, it is as common to hear Spanish as it is to hear English. What's worse are the lengths to which government will go to make this a country where "se habla español." It is a puzzle: in order to become active in public discourse and engage in the life of this land, one must have the ability to read and speak English. It is not open for negotiation.

This is compounded by the shameful advocacy of a deeply misguided few to recognize the Islamic moral code and religious law in this land. The real American has no truck with this deeply inferior and immoral system and requires little other than the grand United States Constitution.

However, for every illegal immigrant that enters this country, there is one who came here through the proper channels, who considers that he or she is owed nothing. Every family that has escaped religious or cultural persecution can begin again here. For those who seek the values, opportunities, and lifestyle of the American—their shot at the American dream—their footholds in the mountain of success are matters of choice and personal work.

The ethnic heritage of a man in this land remains only in his last name, its absence conspicuous in his personality, interests, and moral compass. He is not defined by limits or certain traits of the circumstances of his birth. He, an individual, is what he chooses to be. Unburdened and unfixed. The way it should be.

***

There is outspoken concern held by some Americans that patriotism is no longer as ardent as it once was. And it's awful that it is damn near impossible to find things made in America today. That sure needs to be fixed. But legends, champions, pioneers, innovators, and dreams are still made here. The culture of the world today was made here. It's why little Chinese kids run around with iPhones on rural farms, with their baseball caps on backwards. American patriots should take comfort in the fact that they are only, once more, falling behind their own potential, not behind any other nation. This is America's world, and patriots know it. And thank God for that.

3

Faith

While the rest of the West practices secular humanism as if it were a real religion, many patriotic Americans are fluent in their Christian faith. In fact, the entire American experience is irrevocably connected through Christianity, and religious observance is very common throughout the land. Americans acknowledge God on their money, in their courtrooms, and in their national anthem. Not to mention the Declaration of Independence, the Pledge of Allegiance, and their founding document. *God is everywhere.* John Adams wasn't joking when he said that the Constitution "is designed for a moral and religious people" and that "it is wholly inadequate for any other."[1] Christianity may not have been specifically mentioned in the founding documents of their government, but the Founders demanded religious freedom. Upon further inspection of the Constitution, one cannot help but see the element of faith in the wording, and in the lives of many of its writers.

The Founders understood that a free people cannot survive under a republican constitution unless they remain virtuous and morally strong. And the most promising method of securing a virtuous people is to elect virtuous leaders. Without religion, the government of a free people cannot be maintained. The Founders were right in thinking that then, and they are right today.

Though relativists, secularists, and non-Christians may assert that this is not a Christian nation, they are mistaken. I am unable to imagine a land with a greater priority or passion for Christ. And it's great because it's at the heart of what makes this nation indispensable, different, and exceptional. It's America's secret weapon. Yet, though many may see it, few join the dots to understand its effects. *From everything I see, the central text of the American value system is the Bible.*

This very nation was founded on the Christian view of man and government that prevailed at the time. Sure, not all the Founders were orthodox Christians, but they all respected the Christian worldview of morality and absolute truth (i.e., the "law of nature") and saw it as necessary to remain a free country. But the truth is the prevailing opinion was a Christian view of man and government. The intent to forge a nation under God is clear to any reader of the Declaration of Independence, the Constitution, and the Bill of Rights—America's famous texts. Even the capital of this nation, a city named after the greatest American of them all, is covered with references to God and faith by past leaders of this land. Visitors who see these tributes, walking from one to the other, can feel the Christian roots underneath the soil on which they tread.

It is clear from US history that Americans' civic religion intensifies when they see the effects of atheism or evil; in the decade following the Second World War, patriotism was accompanied by a dramatic increase in civic religion. Think of President Eisenhower, who, in a bid to formally differentiate this land from the godless Soviet Union, added the words "under God" to the Pledge of Allegiance in 1954. Upon doing so, he said, "In this way, we are reaffirming the transcendence of religious faith in America's heritage and future; in this way we shall constantly strengthen those spiritual weapons which forever will be our country's most powerful resource in peace and war."[2]

Christian worship arms the American with fortitude and peace, requisite qualities for any world leader. *It explains the famous American confidence.* The visitor finds that Christianity is consuming; it soothes the cultural soul and heals the national heart. And Americans are cognizant of the curative role religion can play even in internal national matters, like the aftermath of the Civil War and the prejudices associated with the civil rights movement. After the evil of September 11, they turned to it again. They keep turning to it, and every time they do, it allows them not to just dance with broken hearts but to get stronger.

Patriotic Americans have demonstrated the truth of Eisenhower's words and the success of the Christian faith throughout their history. They offer the superb example of their nation, one with the greatest degree of liberty, prosperity, creativity, optimism, success, and peace, as evidence. Americans juxtapose their experience and God-fearing character with those of the avowed atheism of the previous century. Proudly secular tourists may find the religious fervor of Americans humorous, embarrassing, or even nauseating, but they certainly can't deny that where atheism delivered the two most murderous regimes of the previous century—Nazi Germany and the Soviet Union—Christianity has permitted America to be the dynamic torch of liberty and the ultimate citadel upon which dreams of tyranny and oppression are shattered. That's how Americans have chilled the bones and frozen the sweat of men who dream about tyranny.

Nor can it be ignored that the more Christianity eroded in Europe, the weaker Europe became and the less power it held. In every way conceivable. A lesson Americans must note.

***

True to the word of the Gospel, God is omnipresent in this land, to the American and visitor alike. He is there every time the American, or for that matter, the visitor, reaches into his pocket: the national motto "In God We Trust" is inscribed on America's coins and printed on its dollars. The political leaders of this land are incapable of delivering a significant oration without the concluding refrain of "God bless America." This makes outsiders unaccustomed to references to deity in community occasions or public life, feel uplifted, inspired, and included in something greater than themselves.

The religious heritage and nature of this country are exceptional yet provocative. It feels at times that citizens of this nation are permanently set on a collision course with the secular Left ideology, which many of America's allies have embraced. Not because everyday Americans want to, but because they keep being pulled in this direction by international socialists in media, schools, and politics who want to bring America down to the level of every other country. They tell us that no person of any depth could possibly be religious. They say religion has no place in social discourse. See, secularity is a necessity for the liberal agenda because it means citizens are disarmed of virtues and values. Religion just gets in the way and complicates things. After all, the problem with atheists is not that they will believe in nothing, but that they will believe in anything.

Let's be clear. The American can also be religiously diverse. Christianity is not the only religion of this nation, and this is a deliberate consequence of its founding. But in this great cultural melting pot of *E pluribus unum*, the different religions coexist peacefully because of the combined society Americans have fostered. Here, interreligious association occurs daily without a second thought, unlike other nations that are separated within by culture and religion.

The intensity of the religion of this land varies and is largely dependent on location; the two brackets of its eastern and western coastlines participate comparatively less. But even in these predominantly left communities, the East and West coasts, there is still much more religious participation and appetite than in Sydney or London or Toronto. These more progressive communities in America are still molded by the overpowering national sentiment. It is a myth that the religious American only hails from the Deep South of this nation, although there is an old saying in the South: "It doesn't matter how you find religion, as long as you do." In truth, the committed Christians are scattered like seeds in and across every direction. But here's the deal. Even if proud Americans do not speak of God regularly and do not attend church, they still have a silent and deep respect for faith and spirituality; they acknowledge that religion is not for them but appreciate almost to the point of admiration others whose lives are defined by it. Passion and enthusiasm are embarrassing to people of other Western lands, particularly if they do not share the zest for matters of religion. Not here.

Conservative, patriotic Americans are most likely to attend church at least once a week, a powerful contrast to their cousins in the West. Faith is now barren in formerly religious nations, with backs proudly turned on God. The voice of the Church has sunk to a pathetic whisper. Europeans tend to do the "Love thy neighbor" part quite well; you've got a better chance of finding a European who doesn't watch soccer than finding one who goes to church. Instead, they put their hope and trust in the fraud of the multicultural, multi-faith, and humanist state. No blessing comes from following this path. This is plain to see. The financial detonation of Europe is also moral and cultural. Thankfully, and refreshingly, there is a distinctly religious character of the American land, and to many people, the primary reason that creativity triumphs over destruction and hope presides over despair is that the virtues and values of most Americans are seeded in Christianity.

Personal values in America are fortified by Christianity. Proud Americans are lifted and reassured by God, and they, as their past leaders did, seek providential help for their lives and even their nation. It is not uncommon to see an American saying grace in a public restaurant or prayers before meetings.

Conservative Americans engage in prayer, both individually and collectively; they are devoted believers in intercessory prayer because a team of individuals super-glued by the moral imperative of their personal faith will always trump the mediocrity of a team of collectivists. Collectivism, the political principle of centralized social and economic control, insists on the importance of social cohesion, trumping individual opinion and liberty. It is where your life no longer truly belongs to you, but becomes the property of the society you are in, and where you are expected to submit to its values.

Tocqueville had some wonderful insights, but in all his extensive writings on religion in this land, he was at his finest when he offered the following:

> On close inspection, we shall find that religion, and not fear, has ever been the cause of the long-lived prosperity of an absolute government. . . .
>
> There is no country in the world where the Christian religion retains a greater influence over the souls of men than in America, and there can be no greater proof of its utility and of its conformity to human nature than that its influence is powerfully felt over the most enlightened and free nation of the earth.[3]

For all the travel that has carried me to every corner, quarter, and pocket of this land, I can only agree with Tocqueville's opinion. Even today, with Americans having pro-pelled themselves forward with such magnitude and force in all conceivable fields, it is only when one visits the churches and sits in the pews with them that the magnitude of the role faith plays in daily life can be fully understood.

The churches here are incomparable to any I have previously entered. They aren't stoic and cold. Instead they overflow with charisma and drip with life. The sight of worship here is definitely one to behold because another product of America's faith is an uncommon level of emotion during worship.

Visitors are astonished by what they witness, especially if they are used to either no religious experience or to one that is so dull and outdated that it is meaningless. For many Americans, church and faith are very meaningful, and the expression of faith is encouraged. Men and women in some of America's more spirited congregations often celebrate with boisterous and uplifting songs. They sit or stand with hands lifted upward and feet tapping to the rhythm, often swaying back and forth. You cannot attend such a service and not be moved by the celebration of the simple treasures of life. Visitors often say the experience leaves them hungry for more.

***

The church experience is not identical throughout this land; it is largely dependent on denomination, size, and location. But the church of charisma here is a native species. This type of church is often gigantic in size, filled on Sunday morning with numbers unfathomable to the outsider: some thousands, others in the tens of thousands, all with their own volunteers directing traffic and their parking lots filled to capacity.

For all the clear staying power of religion in this land and its innumerable churches, matters of faith are surprisingly fluid. While some inherit their congregation or faith, it is common for Americans to change denominations or switch churches or congregation membership more than once. Chalk it up to the continual American footrace in self-improvement and reaching the finishing line of one's dream and objectives.

While a good religious leader may have a passion to reach others, a great leader thinks like a businessperson in this land. Innovation is so integral to religion here, and it reflects the modern modes of communication. The newest technology in music and visuals is often embraced to enhance the worship experience, no matter the size of the congregation. For churches with large numbers, there are smaller groups, often organized by age or gender or relationship status to ensure a feeling of family, unity, and friendship.

When it comes to matters of personal faith, many Americans have an honesty and a willingness to share their views that I have seldom encountered. When discussing their decision with the outsider to embrace the church and God, they speak solemnly in quiet tones as they recount the traumas of their past and reflect on the changes since their former life ended. As they move on to their current life, their volume increases and their tone gains variance; their speech radiates enthusiasm and projects optimism.

A friend of mine in Australia attended a one-off Christian

outreach event run by the Hillsong Church in Australia some years ago. According to my friend, the pastor was one of the most inspiring and engaging speakers he had ever heard. After he had built his sermon to a crescendo, in front of the ten thousand–strong crowd, he then yelled out, "If you want to be saved, stand up right now! Stand up to be saved! Stand up now!" In a crowd of ten thousand, only three people stood up. This prompted the pastor to say, "Wow. Are you guys a tough crowd or what? I mean, I knew the British were reserved, but you guys take the cake!" While most of the congregation were strongly religious, they refused to stand out from the crowd and publicly express their faith.

But religion is openly discussed by the citizens of this nation. Everywhere in the Western world except America, God has been removed from public discourse. Even at Easter and Christmas, public broadcasters no longer play traditional Christian films. Faith dare not be spoken of; public declaration of faith is considered the domain only of the extreme and the rosary rattlers. When was the last time you heard someone say, "God bless" in Stockholm or Brussels or Amsterdam or Berlin? Instead, it's "Today's reading comes from the Gospel of Marx . . ." Of course, Allah is the exception. Heck, it's downright unpatriotic *not* to speak about Allah all day every day if you live in a Western country. *We mince our words; they mince our people. They* being the fanatical Islamists and those moderates who remain silent.

It must be mentioned that even in America, the chattering classes have claimed a moral monopoly, the very antithesis of a free marketplace of ideas. They see themselves as our shepherds, and us as their sheep. *No, thank you.* Some prefer a society where elites decide what each of us "needs" or "deserves." *But who really wants that?*

Because Americans are free of the chains of totalitarianism, they can communicate their faith fearlessly and frankly, a trait most consistent with the teachings of the New Testament: the spreading of good news. And this is just the common churchgoer.

But it is when visitors are greeted with the educated zeal and verbal artistry of preachers—shaping words to sharpen minds, revive spirits, uplift the downcast, and relieve the vulnerable—that they truly appreciate the effect. The essential ingredients of effective speech are self-belief, enthusiasm, and confidence, and in the culture of this land, religion makes that possible. Non-Americans marvel at how articulate the average American is and at how well Americans present at conferences or conventions. That this could be fostered by a lifelong presence of religion should occasion little surprise, as the modern English tongue was born in the minds of Wycliffe and Tyndale as they set about translating the inaccessible Latin Scriptures into the common speech of England.

Even Alexis de Tocqueville was unprepared for the effects of a society with faith: "On my arrival in the United States the religious aspect of the country was the first thing that struck my attention; and the longer I stayed there, the more I perceived the great political consequences resulting from this new state of things to which I was unaccustomed."[4]

But Tocqueville went further, noting what the outsider today still feels about the correlation of Christianity and the virtue of freedom: "The Americans combine the notions of Christianity and of liberty so intimately in their minds that it is impossible to make them conceive the one without the other."[5]

Where citizens of other lands perceive religion as limiting their individual freedom, the American produces a national amalgam. The mortar and marble of American history—much of it in the nation's capital—reads the same as the American's mind-set: that the Creator is the source of American liberty and that God's sovereignty means that all human authority is delegated. Put another way, Americans believe that their fundamental rights come from God and are therefore inalienable. And one wonders why this nation has led the world and been its greatest force for and source of goodness! It may not make sense to someone who stepped straight out of a faculty office and onto an MSNBC set, but it sure makes sense to the rest of us.

When Tocqueville later observed that Americans must surely hold their faith to be "indispensable to the maintenance of Republican institutions,"[6] he was brilliantly accurate. American faith is, in fact, a great source of democracy. *Yes, Americans mix politics and religion because, increasingly, politics keeps on intruding on their religion.*

***

American citizens are the most self-governing anywhere. Even if they have lost their way, they prefer to struggle through. While they remain at all times optimistic, conservative Americans also accept the sin nature of man, the same belief shared by their Founders. It is also clear that this self-determination has helped create a culture of morality and generosity in this land. Neither the bank nor the government is the American's source: God is the provider.

The American is irrefutably charitable and possesses a heart of humanitarianism and a pulse that beats with philanthropy. When the numbers are counted, the individual charity of this land is truly staggering—Americans give at least three times as much on average as Europeans.[7] This country has historically given the most, and generosity here is usually based on religiosity, not wealth. Conservative households also tend to give more. Citizens here are far more inclined to part with whatever of their money they can afford, if it is in aid of a charity. When it comes to social welfare, Americans favor church and community involvement over government. In order to alleviate the growth and role of the US government, although it grows alarmingly and unnecessarily, it is imperative that Americans care for their fellow citizens and not rely on government assistance. America's answer to social ills is the individual. See, rugged individualism is not some exercise in political nostalgia—it is part of the real solution to the current malaise in America.

***

There is faith in a provident God and a belief that God was an active agent in American history. Time and again, dramatic scenes of history echo this feeling. The first American president, George Washington, got on his knees in the snow at Valley Forge to pray. The words of Abraham Lincoln echoed a sentiment similar to Washington's: "I have been driven many times to my knees by the overwhelming conviction that I had nowhere else to go."[8]

For all the military might at Americans' disposal, it is their steadfast belief that their country serves a providential purpose and that is their greatest weapon. Of course, Americans believe that God is neither neutral nor indifferent to this nation, that, at the least, this country is favored, at best chosen, with a divine mandate. But this assertion drives and frames the civil religion of this country. Only such a built-in conviction can account for the nature of American history, rich with this sentiment—from Benjamin Franklin's suggestion for the Great Seal to portray Moses parting the Red Sea, to the declaration of John Adams that the early settlers of America were "a grand scheme and design in Providence,"[9] to General Washington's bulletproof nature.

***

America also harbors a great love for Israel. After all, the nation of Israel is most worthy of admiration and support, even love. It is an unfaltering democracy and a clarion call for excellence and peace. But as the visitor comes to realize, America is inextricably linked to the state of Israel in many ways, so much so that Israel is an American value. American success and purpose are connected to Israel. Palestine loves death as much as Israel loves life. The key difference is and always will be that if the Arabs put down their arms tomorrow, there would be peace. However, if Israel put down its arms tomorrow, Israel would cease to exist.

Citizens of this land find both political and religious resonance in the providential story of Israel. Conservative Americans interpret the events of the Israel narrative as further indication that the Bible's content can be trusted. To their credit, it is a logical religious position. Think about it: it is beyond remarkable that two thousand years of Jewish oppression and statelessness could be followed by not only their restoration to the Holy Land but also the creation of a deeply successful and democratic state. If you're not on the side of Israel, you ignore the history of millennia.

Americans' knowledge of the Bible means they understand their obligations to the Israeli state and the consequences of abandoning them. This is no diplomatic tie. It's one idea tied to another: America bound to Israel. It's a deep and abiding commitment. It's patriotic to support Israel. It's the syrup to pancakes. The gravy to biscuits. And even war-weary Americans must remember that a strong Israel is the best deterrent to a Middle East war.

It's easy to identify a political connection between this land and Israel as well. President Harry Truman summed it up when he said, "I had faith in Israel before it was established, I have faith in it now. I believe it has a glorious future before it—not just another sovereign nation, but as an embodiment of the great ideals of our civilization."[10]

There are distinct similarities between each nation's values and cultural conservatism. A Judeo-Christian heritage is the foundation of America, and until recently, has been the invaluable defense to moral relativism, a condition that largely robbed the West of its soul. Both are naturally disposed to patriotic sentiment and a fierce desire for sovereignty, contrary to the objectives of the internationalist agenda to transcend borders. Similarities exist in attitude and action too. Both countries have the chutzpah. Neither nation is a pushover, and both will strike if provoked, needed, or left no option. Nothing sissy about them. You mess with Israel, you mess with the American giant. *If Israel cannot exist in peace, none of us can. We are all Israel.*

***

The longevity of the Christian faith is owed, in no small part, to the characteristics of religion in this nation. But I don't believe the brand of faith that exists here can be replicated elsewhere—even in Israel. It relies so heavily on the persona of the American, a product of America's unique culture, intrinsically different from all other people. Only in America.

If Americans continue to comprehend the simple idea that virtue cannot be sustained in the absence of Christianity and that if virtue is absent, then liberty must be as well, I see few ways the citizens of other nations can catch them. Americans' adherence to this equation is their security of exceptionalism. As Tocqueville noted, "Despotism may govern without faith, but liberty cannot."[11] Americans are in control of their destinies. They alone have the key to American despair and tyranny. A nation's cultural and political priorities are influenced by faith. While the Left seek to champion economic equality, America through faith is more interested in underpinning moral self-improvement.

This is America by nature. The exceptions come through Leftist poison. It is deeply troubling that one of the last remaining prejudices acceptable in American society appears to be a bias against Christians. *The war on Christianity is just as real as the war on America.* Even if they're not fully conscious, the Left understand on a visceral level at least that Christianity is at the center of the US exceptionalism web. And it stands in their way. It's why they spend so much time bashing it.

Other words that many in America appear to live by and, in my view, must continue to subscribe to, are those of the great President Ronald Reagan: "If we forget we are One Nation under God, we will be a nation gone under." America is the only place left in the world where its citizens truly believe in breakthroughs and turnarounds and miracles. Faith sees all problems as opportunity. Faith without works is dead. Belief is the key to the door of the supernatural. It is the currency of heaven.

I'll tell you something else the Founders believed: the United States has a manifest destiny to become a glorious example of God's law under a Constitution that will inspire the entire human race. *Amen.*

4

God's Troops

The fight against evil can only be categorized as the noblest act of humanity, and the success of that objective is its greatest achievement. Likewise, the noblest cause and greatest accomplishment of any nation is the same struggle. America has dedicated itself more to this fight than any other. And looking forward, it won't change. None of the global challenges, from defeating terror, to widening economic opportunity, to building a world order based on mutual respect, can be secured without American power and purpose.

The history of the modern world, when taught factually with balance and without bias, affirms the debt of gratitude owed to the people of this land. Without them, Europe would suffer under tyranny, the Asian continent under a single emperor, Australia and New Zealand would be under Japanese control, and the people of eastern Europe would be without a taste of the freedom they have today. America is most proud of her victories. And why shouldn't she be? America has shown uncommon valor against the sword of tyranny. Without her sacrifices and accomplishments, there would have been an almost certain descent of a new Dark Age upon the world. *There's no argument.*

Part of what makes America so great is her military—possibly the greatest manifestation of this land's exceptionalism. And wherever evil threatens the sanctity of freedom, Americans make it their duty to defend. The difference is that in other nations, history has taught that weakness is provocative.

I discovered early in my travels that patriotic Americans consider evil a noun, not an adjective. They hold a dualistic, unambiguous, and black-and-white worldview that colors them and the decisions their leaders make. Americans are always the first to boldly step forward to put an end to the savage marauding of freedom. *Stormin' shores and winnin' wars.* Since the abandonment of isolationist policies, Americans appear to never choose the sideline—always the front line in these matters. It helps that the US military is the finest in the world. America has to always lead from the front.

It is certainly true that at the core of any great nation is a strong military, but the true test of greatness is the cultural weight it lends to its troops. American patriots have a visceral, unconditional love for their armed forces, which is permanently on display. They believe that their troops are God's, carrying out His work. *America is the keeper of civilization.* I love America for its promise of justice in a hostile and cruel world.

The visitor finds that this love and appreciation of things military is far in excess of that of any other society. Where citizens of other countries generally greet their respective militaries with courtesy and platitude, Americans have an incomparable reverence and adulation. Patriotic Americans appear to understand better than any the reality that the few men and women who stand tall are the reason that some in society can stand at all. Every American, it seems, has been touched in some way by the military.

Because of that deep love and respect, it is not uncommon to see Americans in public wave, salute, or signal approval to the men and women in uniform. What a difference from America's Atlantic neighbor, Britain, where British military are told to wear civilian clothing when back home so as not to incite violence, particularly after the gruesome hacking to death of British Army Drummer Lee Rigby in a public place of greater London. In America I have witnessed, on more than one occasion, a civilian approaching a man in uniform and politely interrupting him to express gratitude for his service. But I have never been left more breathless, or felt such over-whelming awareness of American gratitude and pride, than the day I saw an ovation given to military personnel in the airport as I sat at my gate, red-eyed, in the early morning. Each American around me instinctively stood to wildly applaud and loudly cheer until this small band of intrepid freedom fighters with travel bags over their shoulders was no longer in sight. I was numbed with pride. Goose bumps covered my arms. That would never happen in any other country. America gets it. Better to spend one day as a lion than a thousand as a lamb. *Land of the free* because of *the brave.*

I can only imagine the looks on the faces of Europeans

and other international tourists when they encounter the Armed Forces Recruiting Station, directly in the center of Times Square, the "Crossroads of the World." This impressive and patriotic sight sums up just about everything you need to know about America. *What says strength better than that?* I loved it. Heck, I was ready to go suit up, and I'm not even eligible. It's an experience that will never leave me. Could you imagine an equivalent in Sydney or London or Paris? Ah, the things Americans can't appreciate about their greatness until you point it out to them.

Their land's profound militarism sets Americans apart from their Western cousins, even those with the English tongue: the most striking difference is perhaps their gallant Australian ally, who are a martial people if pushed, but never militaristic. It is clear that American patriots see their military as the protector and purveyor of freedom, and it must not be forgotten that freedom is their identity. After all, it is what the first immigrants came here for.

All across this nation, Americans have set up extraordinary numbers of museums, memorials, artifacts, tributes, and military cemeteries—both as a product of the grand virtue of militarism and a masterful method by which to remind a citizenry of its service. It is, for all these reasons, why the military is such an integral part of American life and why it is central to the impregnable fortress of the American mind: confidence, faith, passion, and gratitude. A Korean War veteran once told me about his visit to the local veteran cemetery with his wife to make funeral and burial arrangements; he asked to know the cost for two spaces—and was told he had already paid for it.

Americans express a fierce demand for human rights, albeit in a form very different from that to which I (and presumably other outsiders) am accustomed. Where the outsider is inclined to gain the consensus of the world before commencing military action, Americans believe in the morality of protecting their liberty from the unwelcome intrusion of foreign bodies. And thank God for that. This is a people who are reluctant to rely on the goodwill of the world; they are self-determining. In this way, the teeth of the American form a most stark contrast to the bowed back of the foreign body. Patriotic Americans aspire to lead, while many outsiders wear a badge of hesitation and failure, largely a result, I feel, of their insistent advance or tacit approval of bureaucratic internationalism. The international organizations, which are the impotent brainchildren of the relativist and internationalist, suffer an inherent weakness and are striking only in their capacity for moral destitution. This is the great moral and political difference separating this land from others—outsiders in the last half century have demonstrated a deficiency in fighting evil, a consequence of the alarming dearth of moral clarity in their lands, whereas American patriots are undoubtedly committed to the fight against evil in the world. In other countries, there is nothing like a disposable plastic shopping bag or a politically incorrect football team name to get the blood boiling. That's the moral difference between Right and Left.

I could not care less, nor should Americans, about whether America is liked or popular or understood. Far better than being liked and understood is being respected. Feared, even. That's an ideal context. That's how you keep a country safe. That's how you keep the world safe.

At the heart of the patriotic American lies the strong virtue of service. Whether through the Army, Navy, Marine Corps, Air Force, or Coast Guard, Americans were often at war in the twentieth century and have been continually at war in the twenty-first. I cannot help but feel that this continued participation has had the effects of increased patriotism, fortified morale, and bolstered unity on this culture. In the face of this, I am left to determine whether it is Providence or supreme exceptionalism, or perhaps an amalgamation of the two, that leads to the well-known fact that war devastates and incurs a great setback to every nation except this one. The sluggish here is replaced by the flourish. Even the American economy appears to benefit from war. It is also not lost on me that this nation is clearly blessed in her geography. With Canada to her north and Mexico to her South, Americans know there is remote chance of military attack from their neighbors. Almost uniquely, the United States has not fought a war with one of its neighbors in over a century, allowing its military to focus their efforts elsewhere. This equates to peace through strength.

But my observations are not to extol war. The human tragedy and cost far offset any level of national compensation. Instead, American patriots are unrivaled in their support of action to liberate societies, eliminate threats, and set other lands in a new and improved direction. The price of spreading these virtues to the corners of the world has been enormous and stirs the deepest reaches of the American soul. The patriotic American's emotion while discussing military service and the fallen, bubbles to the surface with pride. Just visit Arlington National Cemetery in this land's capital and you'll feel a somber sense of awe. Both sobering and impressive, this aesthetic delight is extraordinary in size and designed for public and private tribute. My heart wrenched at the sight of the middle-aged American with only a flimsy fold-out chair, sobbing uncontrollably while visiting a lost son. Such observations are common in this land and remind outsider and native alike of the price of spreading freedom.

It must be remembered that freedom does not equal doing the right thing; it means having the chance to do the right thing. Patriotic Americans believe as much in the responsibility to do the right thing as they do in freedom. They are far from perfect, but they and their nation must remain the greatest example of human civilization, and the model to which other nations aspire. America does not need to attend every argument it is invited to, but it must always do what it can to protect freedom. And the scourge of terrorism must be defeated. An act of cowardice cannot be explained or justified; it can only be answered. Weakness tempts people to do things they otherwise would not do. Still, the only good terrorist is a dead terrorist.

Once here, it is easy for visitors to understand why this nation's military is the target of the anti-American. It appears that the might of American military power grates on the jealous outsider, often spawning the unwarranted castigation and intentional smearing of the serviceperson here. *Inequality is the Left's target, not evil.* Whenever I have had the honor of meeting current-serving members of the US military across this nation, from a truck stop in Canton, Mississippi, to the streets of Washington, DC, I have been struck by their decorum and affability. Even when I visited South Korea, it was my experience that they were unfailingly polite and culturally sensitive.

It is seldom recognized that Americans have only ever deployed in response to aggression, not to practice it. In fact, it is most fitting that values-centric Americans have transformed necessary wars of self-defense into campaigns to spread positive values. Notwithstanding America's supreme military capability, its force has only been moderate or measured. And if not, it's been required. Patriots are quick to point out the nation's response to the unprecedented scale and nature of the September 11 attacks as an example of such restraint. It is true, also, that the American military uniform is to the eye of the oppressed civilian what the oasis is to one dying of thirst: the subjugated run *to* it, not away from it. And there are few uniforms in history that boast this effect.

While it is true that there is no other society on this earth that possesses such ideals, there also exists no other nation such as this in history, and people from lands feminized by secularity, big government, and relativism, with all its soullessness, consider any act of aggression greatly abhorrent. It is, with further irony, the words of another outsider, the famed British philosopher John Stuart Mill, that best encapsulates these sentiments: "War is an ugly thing, but not the ugliest of things. The decayed and degraded state of moral and patriotic feeling that thinks nothing worth a war is worse." A respected or feared nation is a commodity of much greater advantage, and in the case of this land, a benefit to humankind. *Coexist* is such a ponytail word.

Many have described Americans as insolent; this may well be true in some instances, but I see little reason to condemn this trait because I see that their insolence in peace translates to their bravery in war.

Patriotic Americans are most protective of those employed in the armed forces and are vigorously opposed to any military budget cuts. And they should be; there are many misguided folk who would nuke the military budget. Outsiders fortunate enough to visit a base, or one of this country's public military colleges, will find it a world all its own, with amazing facilities. These facilities and the personnel who staff them enable many young men and women to achieve their dreams. I cannot help but feel that the military of this nation is integral, and to tinker with its opportunities, size, or spending would be most unwise, as it would, not least of all, radically alter the career paths of many high school graduates.

There is in the US military a necessary ruthless streak, not unique in the context of war but, at first glance, incompatible with the morality and consistency of the American character. The practice of waterboarding and other interrogation techniques at Guantánamo Bay raised the ire of many who regard these techniques as unpalatable and indefensible. Many were outraged at the inconsistency between the invasion of another country on moral grounds and the absence of morality in the interrogations. But a moral justification, right or wrong, agreeable or otherwise, exists behind America's every act. And I must say, I do have reason to see the morality in such actions. I, as a person of principle, do not see actions taken to protect a national citizenry from mass acts of terrorism a violation of America's moral values. Quite clearly, the patriotic American sees this the same way. If we are to accept that our lands are a safer place solely because of America, then surely it follows that no greater morality can exist than ensuring this nation remains strong. Americans believe that a choice between civilized restraint and Western survival is no choice; such a threat must be met with little hesitation. *Don't retreat. Reload.*

The logical view of war as war and a place for no compromise is shared by many. I am reminded of Winston Churchill, the great wartime prime minister of England, and his demonstration of such sentiments throughout the Second World War. He bombed the German city of Lübeck purely to damage enemy morale, planned to mustard-gas any German invasion, and ignored Mahatma Gandhi's hunger strike in 1943. Let me put it to you simply: I am infinitely more affected by the morality of the potential consequences of Western collapse or weakness than I am by the individual human rights of the enemy combatant. *Don't die a virgin—terrorists are up there waiting for you.*

I am amazed at the role of the American military in securing unprecedented reach and power, physical and economic—controlling the air, seas, and space. The chasm in military might between this land and others must be extraordinary. While it is true that America has augmented the size and power of its military with unparalleled spending, this is by no means the only reason for its unprecedented scope. Never has there been a military with a greater tactical or a more sagacious mind. It has immeasurably enhanced the lives of citizen and outsider alike through development and innovation, creating and developing e-mail, the Internet, and the Global Positioning System, not to mention its advancement of scientific and technological research. American military leadership is substantial. It has furthered humans of every stripe, color, and creed, and no one could imagine the world today without these leaps. Look at it objectively: US leadership and engagement are necessary for almost every regional flash point.

The United States military serves to protect and defend not only America and its allies but also every citizen of every land. It stands ready at all times to deploy, engage, and liberate. The American military protects the world. When outsiders suggest that the United States has a selfish and imperial foreign policy, the American patriot's back stiffens, and proud Americans are almost impudent when they declare that it is only due to this nation that *anyone* walks free. *Oh, by the way, if you are free to be a liberal, thank a person with a gun.* It is known that America has, for at least the last sixty years, beginning with the European Recovery Program (the so-called Marshall Plan), effectively subsidized the defense spending of many lands, including Europe and Australia. Having been spared the financial burden of national military defense, the citizens of many of these countries have been the recipients of generous welfare programs by their government officials, to ensure their reelection. It is in this light that I find myself sympathizing greatly with America's indignation, as its generosity often extends to anti-American minorities, their preachers, and organizers of hate within various lands. That means the bloated welfare system of the West that America fosters is the greatest enabler of modern-day Islamic terrorism. Coupled with political correctness, it provides the greatest seedbed for it. It is a sad but most wretched truth, and one for which I foresee no easy solution.

I had, before coming to the United States, heard only from outsiders who had served alongside American servicemen, and all, without exception, spoke with veneration of the practices and code of the great American military. Being here, I can now better understand their claims that these soldiers, in war, are relatively unrestrained by paperwork or regulation. This ensures confidence, clarity, and aggression in the sensory overload of battle and enables them to impart inspiration to fellow soldiers. In fact, it has been confided to me by an accomplished British SAS officer that even when armed to the teeth, he and his soldiers feel only genuine security in the American's presence. We breathe a "huge sigh of relief when the Americans arrive," he told me. *Nothing better than a can of old-fashioned American whoop-ass.*

I had heard of the famous American Marine, a reportedly fearless soldier of uncommon valor. Marines may look ordinary, but there is something in their eyes, even long after they have worn the uniform, that convinces you they will freeze the sweat and chill the bones of anyone who dreams of tyranny.

The emblem and Latin motto of the United States Marine Corps could not be more fitting to its mission, the former comprising the eagle, globe, and anchor, and the latter culturally abbreviated *Semper Fi*, a reference of dearest significance to every patriot of this land.

While the Marine is exceptional, the Navy SEAL of the Special Operations Command is the most elite of American warriors: a man of the rarest talent, dripping with courage. If the man of this land were to have a face of inspiration, it is the SEAL. His mind is a unique confederation of strength, individualism, faith, patriotism, and eternal optimism. As I read the opening and central paragraphs of the SEALs' official philosophy, expressed with the inspirational rhetoric I have come to expect of any patriotic American, I feel the power of its words:

> In times of uncertainty there is a special breed of warrior ready to answer our Nation's call. A common man with uncommon desire to succeed.
>
> Forged by adversity, he stands alongside America's finest special operations forces to serve his country, the American people, and protect their way of life.
>
> I am that man. . . .
>
> I will never quit. I persevere and thrive on adversity. My Nation expects me to be physically harder and mentally stronger than my enemies. If knocked down, I will get back up, every time. I will draw on every remaining ounce of strength to protect my teammates and to accomplish our mission. I am never out of the fight.[1]

These thoughts are echoed by the patriots of this land and in their intuitive understanding that, unless they are confident, they cannot possibly expect others to have confidence in them. For as long as Americans believe in themselves, failure is an impossible outcome. *This is a life lesson, as well as a military one.*

The average American is more acutely aware than any of his or her contemporaries that with great power comes great responsibility. *To whom much is given, much is required.* This awareness coupled with Judeo-Christian values are most substantial and invaluable in humanitarian matters. America's military is the primary vehicle of this work, as food, clothes, shelter, and essential supplies are delivered through the successful implementation of military programs. It is unrivaled in the financial and physical scope of aid. Americans are instrumental in their response to international disasters, such as the cataclysms in Haiti, Indonesia, and Iran in the last decade. Here, once more, America shows its admirable character by providing assistance to nations, many of whose citizens pray daily for America's downfall.

Americans are also the first to respond to outside tragedies, and they are ready to assist with their exceptional equipment and technology, able to help in ways no other country can. In recent times, Americans were the first responders to the worst aviation accident in French history, in which 228 people perished on a national French carrier. France immediately requested that the Americans use their satellite equipment to locate the aircraft and any bodies, and they did, deploying military personnel, maritime surveillance, and patrol aircraft, to participate in the search-and-rescue effort. Still, the French are today among the most vocal anti-Americans of the West, and yet the American soul, a product of virtue and faith, has prevailed. *So much for the anti-American mantra about the nasty, warmongering, morally bereft American.* Americans are always ready to help others and forever first.

With all the aid given, the American people are uncharacteristically quiet on all matters of philanthropy and humanitarianism; they seem intent on receiving scant recognition in what I can only deem a correspondence to biblical instruction that charity never desires or seeks its own praise, honor, profit, or pleasure.

If I dared give advice to the American giant on matters of aid to nations that threaten to be or have proven themselves to be enemies, I would say this: Make it contingent on behavior. Supporters and exporters of terrorism get nothing. People who burn American flags get nothing. That is how the United States can best protect Christians, Americans, and their allies in the Middle East and elsewhere. It's better to be hated for who you are than loved for who you are not.

Patriotic Americans exhibit a greater mindfulness of freedom, which clearly accounts for their freedom lasting more than two hundred years. But this consciousness has the propensity to slowly fade, and while it is hard to identify, there is a slight shift to be observed at this time. It feels as though only a sustained vigilance can ensure the continued peace of this republic; only the replication of the valor exemplified by the US military on the home front will be sufficient for

America's survival. But it is again the prescient planning of American patriots, most reminiscent of their founders, that fills me with deep hope and suggests this land may yet be at the peak of its power.

Patriotic Americans know that their young must possess the identical zeal for freedom so they can take independent action outside of the propagandist classroom. There are countless character-building institutions for American children, instilling leadership, courage, self-confidence, ethical behavior, and sportsmanship. These uniquely patriotic establishments teach the young men and women of this land the essential survival skills of shooting and hunting, furnish relationships with mentors, and condition the child to excel at competition early. These institutions water the earth of American exceptionalism, making it sprout and thrive.

The words of famous American general Douglas MacArthur that rang in the ears of cadets of the exceptional West Point, must resound in the ears of every American, in whatever form their service takes:

> The long gray line has never failed us. Were you to do so, a million ghosts in olive drab, in brown khaki, in blue and gray, would rise from their white crosses, thundering those magic words: Duty, honor, country.
>
> This does not mean that you are warmongers. On the contrary, the soldier above all other people prays for peace, for he must suffer and bear the deepest wounds and scars of war. But always in our ears ring the ominous words of Plato, that wisest of all philosophers: "Only the dead have seen the end of war."[2]

There is not another individual in the world more committed to freedom than the young American man or woman in uniform. These soldiers travel around the world and leave their families for months and years at a time. They sustain horrific injuries, the loss of limbs and eyesight; suffer in silence with memories of atrocities they cannot speak of; and are still prepared to pay the ultimate sacrifice so that someone they do not know and have never met can be free. Their commitment to freedom is matched only by the inspiration they provide not only to their country but also to the people of the world. *The reality is this: in our world, justice can be imposed by one country only— America.* America must never see the world with rose-colored glasses. War is a human constant. It never goes out of date.

America should never permit a situation where its allies are in retreat and its enemies in advance. The fact that some are now questioning if the United States has the proper amount of muscle and resources—let alone intelligence, will, and moral fortitude—to deal with advancing threats is deeply troubling. The arithmetic for foreign policy is simple for the United States: it needs to be good to its friends, and bad to its enemies. That way people will want your friendship. And they won't want to be your enemy. America has and must always arrive at every conflict with a strong but gentle heart. But also, a firm belief that pursuing America's interest benefits the world, and that a more powerful America is not a more harmful world. I repeat: America doesn't have to attend every argument it is invited to. Far better is peace through strength. We learned that lesson. *Thanks, Neville.* An American can be wounded but never conquered—*vulneror non vincor*. God bless America's wounded warriors.

The US military must never be allowed to be tamed, or downgraded. The world will always be dangerous. And America doesn't get to choose its wars, so it must choose to be always ready to counter. Pray for peace, but prepare for war. With any adversary, you must always evaluate his most dangerous course of action and his most likely course of action. But you always act with his most dangerous course of action in mind. Without an overwhelming military, and a preparedness of the Commander-in-Chief to lead the world, a vacuum is created—and will always be filled by leaders with far fewer scruples about using force. A world that is not led is a world where the bullies and thugs take charge. More Ronald Reagan, less Barack Obama, and no isolationism. America is the greatest country in the world. Don't ever forget it, and don't forget the people who can't come home tonight—and those who can't come home forever—who keep it that way. As we watch the flag unfurl, let us never forget.

The Value of Liberty

For most Americans, *freedom* is the first word they choose when they describe their land. It's so ingrained in them that it's hard for me to even conceive of a people more jealous of their liberty. America rightfully considers itself not only the embodiment of human freedom but also the model for individual liberty. For whatever reason, it seems that the American people are almost incapable of taking freedom and their republic for granted, in large part due to the substantial military presence in the national culture. *This is no docile populace.* Americans know that freedom is not free and are quick to remind visitors of this. The idea of freedom in other nations often differs and frequently has a different value. A true American is moved by the enormous price this nation has paid to defend or spread its values and ideals. And an American patriot is prepared to swim against the current, if needed.

Government's proper role in governance (which was derived from the people's individual sovereignty), in protecting Americans' natural rights to life, liberty, and estate, were laid out in the Declaration of Independence and defined previously by the Founders' contemporary, John Locke, who was a tremendous inspiration to Jefferson and many of the Founders. But in other corners of the world, freedom is just a word. In many cases, a dirty word.

Not to an American. The fidelity of the American to individual liberty is exceptional in its sincerity. Yes, the citizens of this land are deeply aware that liberty may carry an unequal outcome; still they remain committed to its pursuit. They approach it with a genuine faith as opposed to the counterfeit devotion common in other lands of the Western world, where commitment to liberty is conditional and only based on the outcome of equality. Visitors are reminded of the nineteenth century's Civil War in the context of liberty, when here as elsewhere, Americans showed the exception that proves the rule where two competing ideas of liberty collided. Coincidentally, past British freedoms that have been lost in today's England have prospered more in America than on their native soil.

Freedom is not only necessary in America; it's contagious. When immigrants to this nation think back on their choice to make this land home, they speak assuredly of the self-determination and system of values present here as though they had not lived one day without them. They breathlessly talk about the opportunity of this nation and explain that this opportunity is only possible with and by the principles of the American society. It is undeniable that this nation is the most highly desired, and because of that, America accepts more legal immigrants as permanent residents every year than all the other nations of the world combined. Yet despite these great swaths of men and women of the most diverse lands and personality, their assimilation here is faster and calmer than it would be in any other community. *Unlike Europe or Australia, where the melting pot has become an angry buffet.* Maybe those who know what it's like to live without freedom and American values are more appreciative of the opportunity to live with them.

But perhaps most fascinating is the Americans' unwritten contract or community covenant between them and those who choose their land. See, America's special. It has no automatic unity. Deep roots of blood or birth do not exist. But the way it compensates for this is both brilliant and unique. The contract appears to be uninterested in the background or beliefs of the prospective American. It's so simple that it only requires that the incoming immigrant exhibit loyalty to the ideals of his or her new country, and it ensures that he or she will be affectionately welcomed. On the surface, this seems like a flimsy agreement, the kind a lawyer would never advise signing up for. But the yields of the great experiment have forged a bond of great strength. The preparedness of Americans to simply rely on the unity of a set of transcendental values to formulate citizenship is great evidence of their propensity to take on great risk for enormous reward. As Reagan put it, "America represents something universal in the human spirit. I received a letter not long ago from a man who said, 'You can go to Japan to live, but you cannot become Japanese. You can go to France to live and not become a Frenchman. You can go to live in Germany or Turkey, and you won't become a German or a Turk.' But then he added, 'Anybody from any corner of the world can come to America to live and become an American.' "[1]

So, what are these values, and what makes them worth dying for? At its most basic, they are those that fortify the patriot and secure unity. Call America simple, but it understands that you need a national cement. *And that ain't multiculturalism.* American achievement is its real national cement, and yes, it so happens that successful integration is one component. Americans understand better than any other people on earth that a strong belief in one's nation and culture is the armor of a successful and confident country. This isn't to say that Americans don't welcome new perspectives or a fresh influence; after all, theirs is a self-made society, and they readjust and renew with great dexterity. But amid this elasticity, patriotic Americans put this nation first, in typically absolutist terms, which is a powerful exterminator of the noxious weed of homegrown terrorism. *If you're an American by choice, it doesn't matter what you were by compulsion.* America must never be a nation that is the mere sum of its parts, but no greater. It must never abandon E Pluribus unum for multiculturalism. The latter is a policy that displays little acknowledgment of America's impressive moral record. Why is it that multiculturalism embraces the value of other cultures while belittling the achievements and characteristics of America's Judeo-Christian heritage? Nationalism should never be subverted, and America should never be invested in separatism of any kind.

Former British prime minister Margaret Thatcher once said that the world has "never ceased to be dangerous," but the West has "ceased to be vigilant."[2] Political correctness has replaced self-preservation, and liberty has gone with it. It is a primary reason the American experience with Islamic immigration has been until now very different from those of England, Europe, and Australia. Historically, Muslim Americans have been less radical and, despite their faith, have put America first. It is also the reason that until the Fort Hood massacre of November 2009 and the Boston Marathon bombings of 2013, we had seen little Islamic homegrown terrorism rear its evil head on American soil.

The value of liberty in America puts it greatly at odds with major elements of the Islamic faith. Where America was founded on life, liberty, and the pursuit of happiness, Sharia was founded on death, slavery, and the pursuit of power. There is no such thing as a reluctant terrorist. And the West's recent tradition to bow as the terrorists bomb must end. Each time the terrorists attack, liberty itself is violated. They come from the desert, but it is we who have our heads in the sand. Admitting people with incompatible cultures is an irreversible decision with incalculable consequences. Muslims must confront Muslim evil. Our war is with their ideology, not their faith.

***

There's a certain youthfulness, almost a rawness, that exists in America, one that might perhaps be found in one's adolescent stage. It's as if these raw elements in the finished product of the individual and culture were the reason American values transform to self-evident truths. I must say, when speaking to American patriots, it often seems as if their personalities resemble that of the biggest and strongest seventeen-year-old star football player of the local school, belonging to a family of committed Christians. Patriotic Americans hold their values as tightly and patently true as would be expected of such a student. Such a character would be far more inclined to fight passionately on behalf of their values than those graying and mature adults whose national pride and recognition of America's greatness have dimmed. *Exuberant idealism is the American way.*

The uniqueness of this land in having been intentionally brought into being should ensure that these somewhat coarse but certainly adolescent trademarks are retained for the life of this nation. True patriots have thus far repelled the external forces of elite culture, refusing to succumb to their utopian temptations and the idea that no set of values is worth defending. But dangers are visible on the horizon. The media-academic corridor is the new big bully in town, and it is every bit as condescending as the aristocracy America's first immigrants left behind in Britain. *But in real America, that dog don't hunt.*

However adolescent these values may appear to be, they have exhibited remarkable and unprecedented staying power. If America were to follow the fate of the Romans, Byzantines, Abbasids, Ottomans, and Khans, or the once-magnificent nations of Old Europe, by disintegrating into the dusk of moral and cultural decadence, there is little doubt that her fall from grace will be the most spectacular and steepest of all. It will be the day darkness covers the world.

One of the best ways to make sure these values aren't threatened is to always be alert and aware. To that end, I must say that Americans in general possess a healthy paranoia—a defense system that they've shown can successfully detect the adversity in what appears innocuous and in what has occurred by stealth. That leaves the cultural beast of relativism struggling to prey here in the American jungle, and it largely protects the American from fateful compromise with the ideologies of other nations that conflict with those of the Founders. The eagle is always watching. *And a darn good thing, too.*

Many citizens of foreign lands, and perhaps some in this one, believe that America is finished. Done. Dusted. Its time is up. The same people would tell you that right now, as you read this, we have entered a post-American era. A post-American world where America no longer calls the shots. *That assessment isn't worth a dime.*

Visitors to this land still sense the grandness of America with their every step. It is impossible to be on this soil among exceptional people without the feeling of exhilaration and hope. After all, a patriotic American excites the soul and senses like no other. It is clear now, though, from the faces of such people, that they are in hard times, and visitors can well see, based on their knowledge of the past, that America is not at its peak; its people could and should be doing much better. This is not to discount the unusually high expectations of the citizens of this land, but it is why the usually upbeat Americans today find themselves with somewhat slumped shoulders. But let's do away with the fantasy: the people who claim the end of the American's cultural dominance are wrong. These are fanciful claims asserted more in desperate hope than objective analysis.

If America is waning, it is because the entitlement state

is waxing. There is a difference between a safety-net state and an entitlement state. One is sustainable; the other isn't. If America continues on its path, it will lose its creative energy, and it will observe even steeper decline in its economy, education, and civility. The quickest way to destroy character is to breed self-centered entitlement. Critics of America complain of its economic inequality. But this country has believed, and should continue to believe, that it should strive for income opportunity, not income equality. That creating wealth takes precedence over the elimination of economic inequality. The truth is that the only track to social justice is building a strong economy that can deliver opportunity. Only economic liberty creates stability. It is the only economic system (with a proven track record) that brings freedom and prosperity to any society that embraces it. I'll tell you this: socialism doesn't end poverty, but it certainly kills opportunity.

But even in dark times when Americans and their homeland are nearing their lowest ebb, the people rise up and draw power from the foundations of their culture. Though this century may impose far greater challenges and graver threats to it than the last, this, too, will surely be an American century. The system the Founders set up generated the cultural capital outlined, capital so substantial that America is always in with a shot, no matter the odds. America doesn't need to be accepted by others; it just needs to accept itself. I want Americans to be convinced, as I am, that pursuing America's interests benefits the world.

Competitive Culture

American culture is open and buoyant. Bold. Exciting. It is also very unique. Success and audacity are what fuel the American heart and soul. People here thumb their noses at restrictions and small thinkers. The greatest disdain is held, not for the state of mediocrity, but for those who aspire to it. Here, historically, there has always been a firm will to win. Eccentricity is praised and celebrated, and the individual is cultivated at the expense of the collective. This is a land where fierce competition is sponsored and an entrepreneurial spirit is breathed. *What American kid wants to grow up and be the* vice *president? Who came second in the hundred-yard dash in the Olympics? In America, if you're not first, you're last.*

It's very easy to develop an emotional connection to the people of America. It's their hunger. There's something in the water. They're open to inspiration because they're inspirational themselves. They buy into the story. They feed off each other. They're confident.

If you want to make history, you have to be in America.

If you desire to be the best, you've got to be in America. If you long to create industries that don't exist, you have to be in America. It's the country that makes the impossible possible. It's amazing.

And it's the only country where success isn't a mirage. *Where you really can do just about anything.* Mostly around the world, your fate and identity are handed to you, but in the great country of America, you determine them. It's why pro-American outsiders like me believe in Americans more than Americans believe in themselves right now. We believe in you. The world believes America is capable of anything. It's why so many people are hostile to it. It's also why so many people would give their right arm to be part of it.

Part of the culture of this great nation is that its citizens possess an air of supreme confidence, which buoys the essential American spirit. It is a powerful machine capable of tremendous precision. *The culture in America, unlike elsewhere, promotes life as an adventure, not an ordeal.* When working at its optimum, humanity fulfills its destiny, the weak become strong, and the strong become great. Americans' national culture has afforded them extraordinary domination: agriculture, industry, and information belong to them. And human innovation translates to inventive genius. The cultural exports of this land reach the corners of the world, and America's scientific discovery is equally limitless. In economics, in science, in culture, and militarily, the land here is grandly exceptional, with the individual setting the standard and the outsider taking action with one eye firmly fixed on the American experience. *Brave hearts, bold minds.*

As I spend significant time here visiting America's many states, it is impossible not to notice how so many industry leaders with flourishing careers are not originally from this country. But the flight of the talented and ambitious from their native lands to America is not novel. Countries that suffer the so-called brain drain can usually expect their best and brightest to pursue their interests in America. It is clear that Americans could not see matters more differently than citizens of other lands. Where the outsider culture, armed with socialistic sympathies, views its best and brightest as a relaxed comfort, a demographic to which little or no responsibility is due, in this country, their American equivalents are the most intentionally nurtured, mentored, guided, promoted, and rewarded. That's why talented and ambitious outsiders gladly make this country their new home. Their appetite for ambition is satiated here, and their dreams of greatness are realized through opportunity. *That's why people cross oceans to come here.*

The national culture of this land is the construct of foundational traits—stout Christianity and individualism. Americans emphatically and repeatedly underline the individual in their appraisal of business, life, performance, and social developments. In fact, it appears that only on matters of national affairs do they focus collectively. This is very unfamiliar to outsiders. Americans are baffled by the vague and undefined concept of teamwork. They do not develop the character traits that would qualify them as team players (unless they are in the military, belong to a professional organization or sports team, or patriotic or civic duty requires them to). Where collectivist doctrine stipulates that no one individual should be greater than any organization, such timid and weak insecurity holds no ground here. The collectivist-minded corporate employer, for example, finds greater virtue in an individual bearing limited talent but an abundant team spirit than in a brilliant and strident individualist. But here in this country, the leeching, Old World belief in the institution, which is prevalent in the English-speaking world and abounding in aristocratic overtures, is a minor influence. Most often the American will glorify the individual to the level where he or she replaces the institution. And let's face it: sometimes someone *is* the organization. *Brilliant individuals are not only more valuable than legions of mediocrity; they are often more valuable than groups that include brilliant individuals.* Our brains excel individually but have a tendency to buckle in groups. This is why we have individual decision makers in business and why, paradoxically, we have group decisions in government.

The culture of this land is also mathematical; the individual operates at his or her optimum level while elevating the collective, thus yielding the identical desired outcome of the collectivist, minus the hesitancy. The primary difference is that Americans accomplish good works naturally, without being subjected to moral judgment and uneasiness about their individual roles within a team. The capacity of dreams must never be discounted, and a dream, much like a prayer, is an inherently personal act. Confiscating the dream of higher aspirations, as the collectivist insists on, is counterproductive. In my mind, this is further proof that the American has it right. *What do you do when your dreams start to fade? You reach for one more dream.*

Americans are exceptional because their roots are profoundly antistatist. Sovereignty is invested in the people, not the state. When sovereignty rests with people, the capacity for human achievement is limitless, as the American demonstrates. This is the ultimate appeal of the American culture: it is a vehicle, powered by the fuel of mainstay values, for the fulfillment of dreams through opportunity and risk. For those who hold local community in high esteem, when the law conflicts with matters of the heart or soul, they are far more inclined to favor grace on their fellow man. *Localism is the great understated virtue of our time, and Americans have it in spades, due again to the brilliance of their Founders. It encourages responsibility and great citizenship.*

Americans are alternately dreamers and realists; they have raised this paradox to an art form. There exists a culture in America that I can only describe as the culture of "yes." It is greatly unique, even to the rest of the Western world, which is more accustomed to a culture of "no." At the heart of a culture of "no," the central attitude consigns the people of that culture to obscurity. Leading pleasant and contented lives, characterized by conservative small steps, such societies have a remote chance of leaving an enduring legacy. *A horizontal linear life has no virtue.* Americans, I feel, have the correct view of life: they are the music makers, the dreamers of dreams, and they know the only pursuit worthwhile is the seemingly impossible one. *Replace upward mobility with downward stability? No, thank you.*

The mind-sets of negativity and mediocrity are abnormal here and are in extremely short supply. *People of other nations are driven by a fear of loss; the American, driven by a desire for gain.* Where caution maims, risk mobilizes. It's the difference between something and everything.

In this candid country, the dream is not merely an internal state of the mind, but a verbal proclamation. Where the outsider, cloaked in secular humanist traditions, equates any words of hope and optimism with delusion, the American greets any grand vision for individual life with enormous enthusiasm and makes the impossible feel possible. While the Western outsider belongs to a culture striving for mediocrity, Americans are unabashed in their pursuit of greatness. *And that's what I love about America, and what the Left hates about it.*

America's greatness also nudges people to be bigger and better, all for the sake of competition. Its people, unlike the outsider, see participation alone as being unworthy of a reward; there is no second place. Competition is everywhere across this great land, and on every level it is inescapable preparation for the real world. Up until recently, the children of this country have been raised to understand the reality of competition, with the emphasis on being the best. But in other countries, teachers are likely to inform their students at the conclusion of a sports game that despite the loss of one side, no winner existed, and that every player, from both teams, had won. It's like the math teacher who awards a student with a lollipop for a wrong answer, as encouragement to do better next time. Every child wins a prize. To them, that's normal. But to most Americans, that's a most delusional perspective. And so it should be.

Competition nurtures strong individual performance, and when the individual performs at his or her best, there is a collective benefit. Americans understand that triumph on the world stage demands internal competition. Their drive to compete is fueled by a correct conception of equality: that equality exists through natural law in the presence of individual inalienable rights. It is obvious that the weakness of a society must surely rest with the defective notions of equality. A word on equality: the Founders were very clear. All things were created by God. Therefore, all mankind are equally dependent upon Him, and to Him they are equally responsible. All mankind are created equal. The proper role of government is to protect equal rights, not to provide equal things. *And this is where the aging hippies and academicians have it all wrong.*

There's also an inherent love of the underdog in this culture. It resonates with the American dream of overcoming the circumstances of birth and achieving. Where outsiders may be supportive of the underdog, Americans harbor that love with true legitimacy; they reward both courage and risk, regardless of the outcome. And where the outsider may not love a winner until he is victorious, the heart of the American is with the individual for his entire journey. It's the only authentic underdog appreciation in the world. *It's Rocky.*

To this end, inspiration has become the infrastructure of this culture. The visiting outsider cannot help but be stunned by the popularity and size of the self-help section of the American bookshop. It is common to see an American engaged in reading an autobiography, biography, or other form of motivational material. Prudent Americans tune their attention through reading, learning, watching, and listening to those whom they admire the most and who have attained the highest levels of success. *Why? To build a vocabulary to overcome great odds.* I find this to be unique here in its frequency and range; Americans must surely be the most open of all people to self-improvement. This practice and predilection is entirely compatible with the exceptional love and celebration of success in this grand nation, and it is bolstered by the belief that people can elevate, overcome, and succeed if only they put their hearts and minds into the effort. The absence of relativism in the American psyche is refreshing. In America, someone is actually worth learning from and reading about—we're not all the same, and the successful person didn't just get lucky.

The rejuvenation of the human spirit is effected by inspiration—an inspired person is an emboldened one. I find that Americans are almost addicted to risk, boasting more chutzpah than people of other nations. *When you fail, you learn to lean on your dreams.* Americans show their acceptance of logic and nature, innately understanding that the need to be challenged is intrinsic to success: without risk, one cannot flourish. The culture that presides is encouraging, supportive, and rewarding of the person willing to risk. *And as a result, Americans don't shut up. They get up.* There is no punishing landscape of bleakness. Just as the great document of the American people, the Declaration of Independence, announces the right to pursue happiness, the cultural attitude toward risk affords a daily protection of this right.

Until now, Americans have always chosen to be survivors, not victims. And this must continue. A great people always choose a victor mentality, not a victim mentality. Americans carry great emotion. Where humans are predisposed to inspiration and dreams of a better life, Americans in particular are equally infused with emotion. The American response to stories of personal victories or triumphant journeys in the wake of tremendous adversity is acute. When speaking to audiences across this country, they react to my inspirational stories of overcoming with exuberance and abandon. For the secular non-American, conditioned to be mediocre and to value inconspicuousness, such outward display of emotion would appear excessive. Yet traveling through this land, I am struck that it is the emotion and soul of the American people that are the source of this nation's strength and global supremacy. *Gotta have passion. Otherwise you're as dry as a piece of toast. No honey, no jam, no marmalade. Just toast.*

The inclusivity of the culture of this land is the root of the famous moniker "the land of opportunity" and the culture of "yes" that clearly exists. All over this world, people and nations alike have clambered upon the head of the American eagle, determined to share in the journey toward opportunity. Through their welcoming nature, Americans ensure that the circumstances exist for true and inexhaustible opportunity. Where outsiders react first with skepticism and suspicion at such hospitality, Americans are almost devoid of suspicion; they accept at face value. Novelty and eccentricity are greeted with genuine inquisitiveness; most telling is the motto of one cable giant in this land, capturing this national sentiment: "Characters Welcome."[1] The reward of an accessible and inclusive society is, to the American people, an immeasurable advantage to both innovation and national disposition since Americans understand that if nothing is ventured, nothing is gained. *It's no sin to be born in the gutter. But it's a terrible sin to want to stay there.*

Americans are often astounded to learn that even in the countries of their English-speaking cousins, the citizen who has distinguishing talents or achievements, perceived or genuine, is resented, criticized, and targeted. Prosperity should never be punished. The non-American culture is unforgiving and critical to the successful individual, designed to eliminate confidence and superiority. It is hostile to anyone with initiative, self-esteem, and the ability to make money. To display individuality, to not conform, to make your own rules, leads to a lack of recognition at best, or a steady personal and media assault at worst. In this sense, these cultures are profoundly leftist. *It is true that the Left love trashing individual achievement, as it threatens their vision.* Americans who visit other Western countries are appalled at how brutally unkind these cultures are to their public figures, and how hateful they are to anyone with a degree of success, perceived or otherwise.

Non-American cultures desire a level society. The statist detests personal success and hates it to be rewarded. These circumstances create mediocrity and failure, and offer no incentive for achievement, inspiration, or opportunity. In these societies, success becomes a matter of personal shame.

This is the opposite of how America treats the high achievers. In America, envy is replaced with deep admiration, respect, and personal ambition. The greatest love of the American is the winner, a sign of success. Any visitor can feel the power the American exerts in every effort to assist success. There can be no doubt associated with it: this country is the greatest of any land for the successful individual. Ever wondered why virtually every major star—sports, film, or music—irrespective of where they hail from, lives in America? Not to mention the leaders of most industries. America has benefited enormously from the brain drain mentioned earlier. *Always prefer death on your feet over life on your knees.*

Americans display a remarkable confidence, particularly in their judgment. I find the old-fashioned "vouch for" most alive in America. Outsiders of Western extraction exercise permanent caution, bearing an apprehensive view that their opinions are only relative and may not be shared by others. Americans aren't as cautious. They are, for the most part, averse to negativity, equating it with learning to function in your dysfunction. The outsider's culture, coated with negativity, cultivates loud and effective jeers at success from the sidelines by envious individuals, bursting with disillusionment, to the detriment of the successful individual. Often, it resembles a lynch mob. But that negative voice has little or no place in a positive culture and is drowned, or at least matched, by rallying forces of support. It is most certainly the case here in America; its people love the winner and the state of success.

There is an all-powerful spirit of progress here. Tocqueville's words are truer than ever: "Man is endowed with an indefinite faculty of improvement . . . forever seeking—forever falling, to rise again—often disappointed but not discouraged."[2] I find that the American's mind still bears great resemblance to that of which Henry Adams wrote in reference to the earliest American settlers: "a mere cutting instrument, practical, economical, sharp, and direct."[3]

With success, the true promise of opportunity is measured in accessibility. America gives the greatest number of citizens the chance to succeed. While the right to the "pursuit of happiness" is no guarantee of happiness, the right to pursue it is assured. Americans are enrobed in this right since opportunity relies upon freedom; and these people, the freest of them all, offer it through their physical landmass, population, and national exceptionalism. *Spread across families, towns, counties, and states.*

Americans have a visionary culture that is cognizant of the need for the achievement across generations which earmarks the future generation for focus. The people of this nation, more than any other, believe the mentor to be the greatest agent in this mission, and mentoring another is nearly considered a patriotic duty. In America, it is common practice to mentor up and coming leaders. It's part of the big picture view embraced by American culture; that it is vital for the continued success of the nation that future generations receive the baton. In other countries, this selfless act and patriotic thinking is almost non-existent. Self-interest and short-termism are the fruits of the secular society with the socialistic keystone. They will only keep you down. But the act of mentoring lifts both the giver and the receiver.

Mentoring even finds its way into the family, in the way American parents take ownership of their children's future. From a young age, Americans are made to understand their lives are carved by their own hands, and they must be prepared to journey companionless. As they start their own families, they become more detached from their greater family, conceding further protection and assistance, unlike the European. Though scary and unfamiliar at times, this action bathes the American's subconscious with self-reliance.

In other cultures, citizens absolve themselves of the responsibility, ceding such duties to the government. Parents in other cultures don't think to endow the future generations with grand dreams, which only yields a cycle of permanent inertia. This naturally leads to patriotic drought and serves to exacerbate a fragmented society with no future. In comparison, the mentoring culture extends to academia, with the college mentoring programs of America unrivaled by even the best international universities. Even the leaders of industry are more accessible, approachable, and accommodating to the young aspirant than any of their equivalents in other lands. *In other Western countries, you need to belong to a perceived minority to get mentoring or assistance.*

With all the good poured into others, there's a strange juxtaposition of characteristics at play. The tremendous confidence of Americans is birthed by faith, patriotism, and success. Americans, the most powerful of people, are also said to be the least humble. To an outsider, confidence is automatically seen as arrogance. Those who speak highly of themselves and are active in their own promotion are detested in other cultures, yet Americans consider these ventures as routine, entrepreneurial, and essential to survival.

I find that the people of this nation are the least envious of others, and I can only conclude that it is their healthy pride and religious influence that prevents this envy. This leads to another paradox of the people here. A deeply religious people in comparison with other nations, they are very proud. It is perhaps here that they exercise their most pragmatic element, sensing that rightful pride is an efficient and sufficient defense to envy, which is a stone's throw away from the stream of servility. Though they are proud, they are also humble. Conservative Americans are people of humility in their interpretation of life and events, and because they are guided by their faith: they know, despite their self-determination, *they* are not in overall control.

***

The American child is the apple of the cultural eye. From the moment of birth, children here are given greater freedom than their outside counterparts, and their individuality blossoms. As visitors observe American parents interacting with their children, they find that public encounters prime the child for interacting with others and instill supreme confidence. The five-year-old boy or girl of this nation abounds in confidence, a strong contrast to his or her equivalent Western peers.

A most interesting phenomenon grows at a fast rate here: the idea of homeschooling. A popular method of education, it is proof of America's exceptional focus on its children. While outsiders are convinced that the state is, and should be, the controller and shaper of a child's life and belief set, Americans chisel their belief in stone that a child's parents bear ownership and responsibility for his or her general education. Homeschooling is the fundamental expression of individualism in education and is, therefore, American to the core. Not only that—it is another incredible illustration of the American ability to use its nation's founding values as a solution to a problem. With the public education system and cultural institutions carrying the water for the Left, homeschooling is an individual-generated response. It is precisely this kind of response, and capacity to problem solve, that gives me enormous hope for America's future. *This is why you can never count America out.*

Symbolizing an open culture in which the parents have the choice to either educate or engage a private tutor, homeschooling is available to all the economic classes of this country. The phenomenon is still in seed form and has not yet been witnessed in full bloom. But it is a matter of fact that many European families have sought asylum here in this land because they have been persecuted for their desire to engage in homeschooling, since other governments wish to determine the manner and method by which their nation's youth are trained. This land of the free upholds the natural path, encouraging parents to make decisions regarding the upbringing of their children. Perhaps it is because Americans understand the consequences of the government, rather than individuals, raising the next generation.

***

Some Americans become devotees of media personalities with the same fervor that they may have for a product or brand. It is true that Americans consume the entertainment media with an almost religious fervor, convinced of the major players' judgments due to their personal feats. These public displays of confidence play into the outsiders' assumptions of the American as being totally devoid of any critical analysis. These public displays of confidence feed the outsider's presuppositions about the American that a critical mind could never tolerate such fervent worship. But it is clear that the disparity between Americans and outsiders is due to the divergence on matters of success, emotion, and aspiration. People here see their best chance in life as paramount, seeking a model of success to aspire to. Emotion, hope, success, and optimism—the ingredients of the American recipe—are misunderstood by the anti-American and the outsider. Indeed, there is a great degree of necessary skepticism in patriotic Americans. They overwhelmingly favor their own judgment, seldom having faith in the expert opinion of others. I have only pity for the person who attempts to dictate to them. This is not to say Americans do not defer to professional judgment or respect the authority on a given matter; it simply means that their fierce sense of self-belief and distrust in the elites gives them a wary skepticism.

Americans are very opinionated and may be best described as unashamed extroverts. Thanks to that, the cancer of political correctness is unable to metastasize on any significant level here in this country, at least to the extent of other countries. It is true that America's Western partners do, in their own nations, officially declare the freedom of speech through law and right, but such proclamations are disingenuous. Freedom of speech in America is genuine because, in this land, people generally speak their minds without fear of recrimination or repercussions in society or career. The society that allows its citizens the freedom to speak their minds but punishes, ostracizes, dislodges, and derides—with negative impacts to employment and reputation—devalues the greatest freedom of humanity. Americans are the only people with an authentic and indubitable guarantee to the freedom of speech. Alas, this is changing. It's now more dangerous to be a public figure than ever before. It's also becoming perilous, even in America, to say something that may ruffle feathers or rub the wrong way, and fear of litigation is paralyzing tongues. Scarcely a day goes by without a radio personality "who said the wrong thing" being compelled to apologize, or a television star who criticized someone is forced to resign. Just ask poor old Phil Robertson and the great patriots of the Duck Dynasty.

***

Americans are philanthropic in nature, a feature of the economic and social prosperity of this nation. I find that in this land, homes and pocketbooks are open to the needs of the elderly, handicapped, and orphaned more so than in any other nation. Philanthropic blood courses through the cultural veins here, first injected by the Christian faith then manifested in the "Golden Age" with the great industrialists and bankers of this country, such as Rockefeller, Vanderbilt, Mellon, Carnegie,

Ford, and others. And today, there's Bill Gates of Microsoft, whose acts have paved the way for significant advances in global health and education. But philanthropy happens everywhere across America. In Bastrop, Texas, some thirty miles outside of Austin, the Annual Brent Thurman Memorial Bull Riding is an annual rodeo organized by a mother who lost her son in a tragic rodeo accident. Today she dedicates her life to helping intellectually and physically challenged children by holding this event to raise money for them. In New Orleans in 2009, I was hosted by the president of St. Bernard Parish, a parish southeast of the city. It was one of the parishes most affected by Hurricane Katrina. After being given a tour and seeing the devastation to both the city of New Orleans and the parish, I was invited to join the parish president to address a group of high school student volunteers from Illinois. These American teenagers were sacrificing their summer vacation to come and help restoration efforts within the parish. I was moved as I saw these teenagers at the end of their stay, visibly tired and many covered in paint and other house materials, sit and be graciously thanked for their efforts. When the parish president opened up the floor for casual questions, I was struck by the quality and perceptiveness of questions these students asked and by their deep concern about the long-term impact of Katrina. I have no doubt the equivalent happened after Hurricane Sandy. That's just the way Americans roll.

The palpable effects of such humanitarianism are felt all across the nation, and it is no surprise that the most generous philanthropists and the most munificent foundations are

American. I find American donation patterns interesting. People here give with equal generosity to both secular and religious causes, both democratic and cultural. Americans are forward thinking, most willing to help another person because they see it as critical to defending their own independence. And where help is offered cheerfully and without request, there is no feeling of debt or loss of dignity.

For all of the above reasons, I conclude that the attack of the anti-American, while veiled as targeted criticism, is aimed at the heartbeat of the culture of values. For as long as this country exercises fidelity to its blueprint of the Constitution and the Declaration of Independence, thereby remaining true to her values, there is scarce evidence to suggest its reign can or will be limited. *Don't let the people of other countries who gave up on their dreams talk you out of going after yours.*

The culture war is the ultimate ball game on the soil of freedom. Americans must remember that in the event of defeat, no other America exists as a savior, and life as the Westerner has become accustomed to will also most surely perish. Turn on that dream machine, America. And always live by the words of National Speakers Association founder Cavett Robert: "While I can run, I'll run; while I can walk, I'll walk; when I can only crawl, I'll crawl. But by the grace of God, I'll always be moving forward."

Keep on dreaming, America.

The Land of the Self-Made Man

Americans conduct business in an exceptional way. It is well known that this country is the prime engine of all the economic growth and prosperity of the world. It is also certainly true that one of the greatest accomplishments of any great nation is its ability to spread its culture and values to faraway lands and people. Americans have achieved this without parallel. *A global middle class would not have been possible without American power and purpose in the last sixty years.*

Business and employment in this land occupy the highest echelons of this nation's thought pyramid. Americans not only find their worth but also pursue their happiness and opportunity through their careers and a belief in wealth creation—fundamental to the American experience. *But be wary of liberals; they have never met a regulation they didn't like.*

Because of this, we label American businesspeople entrepreneurs and entrepreneurial innovation as the most distinguishing currency of nations. Fortunately for the American people, these values have been stenciled onto the sheets of their history for generations. They have no greater companion than their most prized documents: the Constitution and the Declaration of Independence. *Of, for, and by the people; not of, for, and by the government.* Innovation often thwarts crisis; it lifts the spirits and encourages a free-thinking mentality.

Americans believe that the challenges of this day will be the victories of the next. In fact, many of the nation's most exceptional business innovations were born in the most economically inhospitable times. Several corporate giants are substantive proof: Microsoft, Hewlett-Packard, General Electric, and IBM. This is easy to explain: the absence of self-confidence inhibits creativity and risk, a deficiency from which Americans do not suffer. They are a most self-confident people and are correspondingly creative and risk-prone. *American self-belief has always been and should always remain a force of nature.* Americans believe in their vocations; they are always seeking a life of meaning. Employment gives them reason and definition, and they thrive on effort. There's also a deep personal pride in their work. It's what happens when government isn't God, trying to control everything.

Service is an enormous priority of the businesses here. The act of tipping is to many outsiders, at first, a most peculiar custom. Hospitality employees of this nation often rely on tips to make ends meet, as the industry has been engineered to offer low hourly rates. It is the American's theory that the income of such employees is uncapped, which provides an enormous incentive to perform for individual rewards. *No limit on potential.* It shouldn't be a surprise, then, that the service offered in the private sector here is exceptional. American employees, typically greeting their customers with a friendly smile, exert considerable effort to be helpful, exude competence, and provide the best experience to every patron. Tipping also proves a flourishing humanitarian spirit: people's moral values and Christian influence are reinforced each time they provide a tip because they are reminded of the need to care for their fellow citizens in the community. *Brilliantly and breathtakingly American in every sense.* Not one other country on the earth has tipping as such an integral part of the economy.

It is said today that this country is the greatest on the earth in which to conduct business. It's the land favored most by the entrepreneur and business owner, including those from other nations. History shows a healthy mix of capitalism, competition, and innovation. Even the climbing entrepreneurs and self-starting businesspeople of other lands renew their dreams here, in the absence of the cumbersome bureaucratic processes and cost-prohibitive matters they were accustomed to. These unique circumstances truly liberate the wings of the entrepreneur. But the most essential capacity of man is to dream. It is essential and nonnegotiable. Without it, mediocrity is guaranteed. And nothing is more un-American than mediocrity. It's why you only ever hear about the American dream. It's still the dream of millions around the world. *Ever heard of the Swedish dream? The Canadian dream? The French dream? Didn't think so.*

As stated before, competition is a natural human circumstance, and a most beneficial one. From the politically correct

view of America's Western counterparts, aside from an organized professional sport, competition is morally questionable,
since it promotes inequality. The exceptionalism of this nation
lies in its unfailing commitment to competition in all arenas
of life, but most spectacularly in her private sector. I have
encountered fewer fiercer forces than the corporate and capitalist sectors in America. It is a matter of course that in the life
of the American business or company, it is forced to rediscover,
revitalize, reimagine, and remake. Such are the consequences of
robust competition and perpetual threat, and such is the self-
made nature of the society in which the business finds itself. In
such societies as this, innovation becomes intrinsic, benefiting
the consumer. The great inventions for which Americans are
renowned, and every school kid could once recite—steamboat,
telegraph, steel plow, reaper, telephone, electric lightbulb,
phonograph, and assembly line—all offer evidence of the
unprecedented and exceptional innovation that has delivered
widespread wealth through technological advances. In today's
world, the use of American inventions is overwhelming. Everyday life involves the use of some American technology, whether
it is the credit card, the jumbo jet, anesthesia, MRIs, cable
television or laser. I could go on for more pages than are in this
book. Whenever I speak to high schools across the country, I
always urge students to google "American inventions." It's fun,
and they love it. American enterprise is strong.

All over this nation, at any one time, visitors are liable to
detect the unmistakable whirring of the business engine. Entrepreneurship and innovation are far and wide across this land,

even in the unlikeliest of territories. From the produce stores of the Amish in Pennsylvania, to the six-year-old in Memphis performing gymnastics on Beale Street, to the lemonade stands of the ambitious young girl in the neighborhood street of central Illinois, initiative transcends geography, culture, or style.

The consumerism infused in the American people demands entrepreneurship, and it is delivered with relish. Coca-Cola can be purchased in more than two hundred countries, and McDonald's has more than thirty thousand locations worldwide. What can I say? *America knows what cranks your tractor.* Visiting the World of Coca-Cola in Atlanta is a capitalist's dream, and an experience I will never forget.

Yet the successful entrepreneur of this land is often more likely to have a checkered past than not. In a land of risk and measureless opportunity, it is common for the inordinately successful businessperson to have been bankrupt at one time, perhaps even more than once. But the American capitalist benefits from redemption, optimism, and a prevailing reluctance toward judgment. Genuine zeniths of achievement require the chasms of failure to have been crossed, and to that end, Americans not only tolerate the recovering entrepreneurs, they celebrate them. *Growth comes only when the seed is buried in dirt, covered in darkness and struggles to reach the light.* More than this, I find that the greater the depths plunged, the higher the esteem for those who have fallen and have gotten back up. A mistake or failing is most easily redeemed in this land. In such a nation of risk-takers, such a public response is most compatible and most reassuring to the human condition, spurring

Americans to push the boundaries of their own exceptionalism in the wake of their seemingly unlimited chances. A vision without execution is just a hallucination.

While some successful people have little to no education past high school, American universities are exceptional in supporting the individual and his or her entrepreneurial quest for success. Nearly all the beasts of the information age were spawned in the computer labs of such educational providers across the land, including Google, Microsoft, Facebook, and Hewlett-Packard. The role of Stanford University in the story of Google is particularly heartwarming, with its financial investment stake in Google and the continual encouragement and support by university administration and staff. This is not to say that college is compulsory for success; four of the greatest companies of the world today were founded by college dropouts Bill Gates, Mark Zuckerberg, Michael Dell, and Steve Jobs.

It was with great interest that I toured Hamburger University, the training facility of McDonald's Corporation, located in Oak Brook, Illinois. An entire university, covering eighty acres of land, is dedicated to training McDonald's personnel, and it teaches people from more than 119 countries. This type of institution could only ever be found in America.

The general energy and optimism in America spill into the workplace. It's an irrepressible environment, a whirlwind of words, ideas, and energy. Employees are invested in the companies for which they work. They speak of their workplaces often with great reverence, as devoted fans might speak of their favorite sports team. The encouragement to speak and act freely means the people of this nation are unreserved and passionate, and why they are unashamed to advertise their places of employment. It is also true that Americans are more inclined to respect their superiors within the workplace than their outsider counterparts may be. The praise of an employer in such a context is powerful, engendering a more harmonious relationship.

The business here mirrors the American's desire to be the best. While the outsider is unaccustomed to self-promotion, the American largely embraces it and is its greatest practitioner. In the truly free society in which government is limited and individuals have only themselves, their families, and their churches on which to rely, such promotion is not only beneficial but also necessary for survival.

In my travels through this nation, I witnessed the ingenuity of the private sector firsthand. I toured the Beistle Company in Shippensburg, Pennsylvania. The Beistle Company will soon celebrate its 105th birthday, and it holds the distinction of being the oldest and biggest party manufacturing company in the world. A producer of hats, napkins, confetti, stickers, wall decals, and all party paraphernalia, and a distributor to hospitals, military, and schools, its scope is enormous. A family-run company, it has endured for over a century, and its story is typical of the American spirit. When all of its competitors moved their manufacturing jobs to China, Beistle made a commitment to protect American jobs and said simply that it would operate with exceptional efficiency to compete with China. Its employee count is extremely low. Employing some 370 employees, with a combined facility size of nine hundred thousand square feet—its size is breathtaking. The ingenuity of the engineers who designed the complex machines is astounding. The care that its employees take to ensure the absence of fault in all products, by individually assessing each, symbolizes American excellence in quality.

Performance reigns supreme in the American workplace, and the mediocre employee here has no place in the fierce and unforgiving landscape of the corporate world. Here employers encourage their workers to develop entrepreneurial flair, to compete, and to exceed their potential; and employers are, from what I have seen, liable to reward such performance accordingly. This nation is advantaged immeasurably by the thrift of its people: the old Protestant work ethic is still very much alive.

America is the home of the franchise, and its greatest export is the unabashed American capitalistic nature. This exported entrepreneurial spirit has enabled people of all nations to own and run a business, simultaneously spreading the most cherished values of freedom and individualism to virtually all corners of the world and bringing to fruition the opportunity for the pursuit of happiness. *Only this nation could have developed a right that so embodies the values it espouses.* More than that, business concepts founded in America, such as personalization of services and employee motivation, are now part and parcel of business and trade around the world.

Americans connect and collaborate like no other people. Their pace is frenzied and their actions immediate, with no second wasted. They are the ultimate multitaskers. Americans are proactive, persistently seeking each new connection or opportunity, oftentimes with their business cards and personal technology as their only essentials. They are born networkers; I can think of no other industrialized country where business networking is as conspicuous as it is in this land. *Fast-paced and high-octane.*

America's networking capacity is ideal in this rapidly developing, technology-driven globalized economy. I find Americans thoroughly addicted to their technology, and they have selflessly and unwittingly imparted their technological innovation and expertise to the outside world. Motivated by their values and desire to help others, their advances have enhanced humanity and businesses everywhere. The remote country town in Western Australia is today the neighbor and business partner of the fishing village in India. The businesses of this country are not without their weaknesses, but even America's internal weaknesses end up strengthening the world. One of America's blessings to the world is free enterprise, and it is one, which encourages and lifts. Americans' predisposition to take risks is not always rewarded, but with the people here always recovering quickly when they fail, they are capable only of increasing their exceptionalism. *It's only when you risk everything that you get somewhere.* Throughout America's history, ranging from financial crises to war, the American boomerang has been ever active, proving that a resilient people and a resilient country can rise to any occasion and stay ahead of the innovation curve.

Constitutionally Limited Government

mericans have a keen interest in and appreciation for their democratic beginnings. It was the Frenchman Tocqueville who made the first outsider observation of the remarkableness and exceptionalism of this people's ability to come together to meet a common objective. This grand observer opined further that this capacity and appetite bred an active political and civil society, effectively safeguarding selfless patriotism through these acts of unity. While the land today is vastly different from what he found, it may certainly be said that Americans continue this tradition of collaboration, more so than any other nation's citizens.

Americans carved their exceptionalism early by choosing a Latin derivative for the name of the legislative assembly known as Congress, from *congressus*, a reference to the active process of having come together. This is in stark contrast to the majority of other nations of the West who favored "Parliament," a reference to a mere place of speech. *Not that it has helped America lately!*

The American people harbor a fervid, almost blazing distaste for and mistrust in government. Their putdowns of government can be withering, and they extol the virtues of the limited government at the drop of a hat. The people of this land are fluent in the simple inverse relationship of reality: with the growth of government comes the reduction of individual liberty. The only aristocracy that exists in the society of this land is one grounded not on birth or need, but on individual courage, effort, and vision. Americans are lifters, not leaners. Their government should stop hustling for the expansion of the welfare state. For the record, most succinctly stated, the purpose of government is to secure our liberties. *Period.* Individual liberty is an essential ingredient for any fair, prosperous society. Insistence on big government and centrally planned, highly regulated societies, and the modern statism they produce, must be definitively rejected. The American state has efficiently nurtured creativity and innovation by allowing enormous scope to its citizens in pursuit of these efforts. Creativity and innovation are wanted. This scope, first envisioned by the Founding Fathers, is the ultimate characterization of the American republic and her people. Where the outsider feels limited or constrained by bureaucratic interference or the need for government approval, Americans are empowered, knowing success is contingent only on them. Here, life is about kicking butt, not kissing it. Of course, God is always in control, and His plan trumps everything; but within this culture, an individual's control of his or her life is at its highest.

This nation is a republic, not a democracy. Unlike the

numerous democratic forms of government in the West, where the outsider as an individual has no protection against the unlimited power of the majority, America's form is a constitutionally limited government with the intent of controlling the majority to protect the individual's God-given and unalienable rights through a written constitution. Religious liberty is the foundation of democratic freedom, and Americans understand this. To study and observe the formation of government here is to realize its main elements spring from a predominantly Christian perspective. As Thomas Jefferson said, "The Bible is the cornerstone of liberty . . . Students' perusal of the sacred volume will make us better citizens, better fathers, and better husbands."[1]

Americans are highly prejudiced in favor of democracy and free will. They are also aware that a nation requires just two generations of utopian statism before she incapacitates herself beyond recovery. I have found that Americans understand, to their great credit, that at its core, utopianism is profoundly anti-democratic. The greatness of the American system lies in the nature of its citizens. Their conception of liberty is different from the self-appointed intellectual guardians of the world today. They see it as the supreme value. An informed citizenry is the bulwark of democracy, and they are the best insulation to the handwringers and bed wetters in D.C.

Americans understand that the government is a far worse employer than the private sector, and that it cannot create net jobs, but most certainly can destroy them with regulation. An American's anchor is self-belief, family, and faith; the outsider's is government. Where a true American's belief is in life, liberty, and the pursuit of happiness, a European's view is debt, deficit, and the pursuit of dependency.

The size of government is inversely proportional to its citizens' satisfaction. If failure is not allowed, then how meaningful is true success? Americans have the right view: nothing worthier exists than the glory of human accomplishment. This pithy little maxim says it best: "We make a living by what we get, but we make a life by what we give."

The American's identity is the most malleable of things; it is a choice he or she makes. In similar fashion, the bamboo that bends is stronger than the oak that resists. Americans are limited not by their cultural ancestry, genetics, or their parents' success, but by their own imaginations, hearts, and desires. They value productivity more than any other people; inaction or mere existence is for the mediocre. This innate love of productivity means Americans are more likely to seek and build their identities through their work, which often leaves the unemployed or retired American a most forlorn sight because the absence of work erodes the sense of worth, which is crucial to the psychology of the human.

The connection of the republican democracy with laissez-faire economics first posited by the great Scottish pioneer of political economy, Adam Smith, is most alive in this great nation. It was Tocqueville who first noted that the American was unfazed at the prospect of people living in accordance to their earning, at the mercy of the marketplace. Each individual should be given the opportunity to succeed economically without interference from the state. See, the industrious American prays for a bigger back, not a lighter load.

Self-reliance is the great nemesis of the powerful government. This is why conservative Americans are fairly resolute in their obstruction of the advancement of socialized health care, housing assistance, and unemployment benefits. While there are understandable exceptions, their values are wholly at odds with these programs. Where others see human rights, conservative Americans see privilege. They know that government welfare encourages a culture of victimization. The government and politicians are all high on the same drug: taxpayers' money. More than that, the government cannot love, cannot teach responsibility, cannot be a parent. Conservative Americans get it. At the core of liberalism is the idea that government is a great mediating force, acting on behalf of the national electorate to balance the competing interests of people. But the government record is not great, and the idealized American doesn't buy it, even though other Westerners do. When the welfare state exists, people end up taking less and less responsibility in all areas that the government provides support. Your stomach might be full, but your soul is empty.

Americans have an immovable fixation on the future: there can be no better tomorrow if all you do is think about yesterday. They appear neither stoic nor resigned to any particular fate. Instead, they consider destiny a location of their own choosing. Improvisation and adaptation are the key tools of the American workshop, the contingency of change ever ready on its top shelf. The most notable example of change was the American response to domestic education in the wake of the Soviet launch of Sputnik, the culmination of which was a comprehensive whipping of the Russians by the National Aeronautics and Space Administration (NASA). And today is perhaps the time when Americans would benefit most from a major national achievement of similar proportion. It is appalling that an American was last on the moon more than forty years ago, and that today the Americans rely on the Russians to take them to the Space Station. Financial limitations given American debt are understandable but space not only carries with it an essential symbolism, but an intellectual infrastructure. Fewer entitlement programs; new space programs. Space achievement must be something America once more looks at, as a vehicle to unite and inspire.

The American political system is truly a sight to behold. Inspiration, individuality, independence, and opportunity are the flavors of the political ice cream. Outsiders bleed in disappointment at their political choices and weep tears of pessimism for their democracy. But Americans are always upbeat, believing that their ballots and those of their fellow patriots can and will effect any change desired. The political style is charismatic, not transactional. The struggle of genuine ideas and philosophical differences is still alive here, unlike in the lands of England and Australia. The American people's optimism has ensured that they have not embraced the view of other English-speaking lands that people cannot change and that government is there to just manage and finance the status quo. Instead the philosophical fight and culture war rage here as Americans believe they can win hearts and minds, refusing to accept the view that people cannot be changed. Anything is possible in America.

The citizens of this proud nation are addicted to the idea of a genuinely free election. They put up, for election, propositions and almost every position available in this society, from the school board to the town dogcatcher. In other lands, the police force, the local school, the hospital, the cemetery, waste collection, and all such matters are the territory of the bureaucrat, with very limited oversight by the politician.

These decentralized democratic traditions of America today were those that Tocqueville so admired because they were the obstacles to tyranny. Americans seem to have always understood that government can only do them, their culture, and their community harm if it is able to reach them. This is why they have always insisted on voting for their judges, their police, and their schools. The localization of power is their defense mechanism. As with the right-thinking people of all nations, they desire to be represented, not governed. Limited government feeds its citizens' dreams and starves their fears. The devolution of America to a European model will see some of life being drained from life. Needs might be met, but there is no deep satisfaction. Nineteenth-century political philosopher John Stuart Mill explained the dangers of big government: "A government with all this mass of favors to give or to withhold, however free in name, wields a power of bribery scarcely surpassed by an avowed autocracy, rendering it master of the elections in almost any circumstances but those of rare and extraordinary public excitement."

The gateway to a nation's liberty is the people's choice to cast a vote. Without it, the democratic system is little but a hollow roar, an affront to the cost of blood and treasure sacrificed for freedom. Many of the outsiders' countries compel them by law to vote, with the looming threat of financial penalty gnawing at the soul of their liberty. Americans gladly volunteer their votes. The outcomes of the system patently espouse the American culture of independence, individuality, risk, optimism, opportunity, meritocracy, and freedom. These ends are achieved in this land through the presence of the genuine political movement, the culture of giving, the primary election, and the medley of free and unfettered opinion. So great is America's obsession with this process that its citizens even vote with their feet—moving to where they want to live and work.

The American system is colorful, presenting a smorgasbord of viewpoints and debate. If Americans are unable to freely express an opinion or be dissentient to party policy without fear of retribution, they become irate and effect change. Elsewhere, any individual defiant of these parameters is persecuted by the media and establishment alike, branded a cowboy or rogue or maverick or renegade, and derided for a lack of team play. More often than not, that individual is excluded. Yet mavericks here are not marginalized or expelled in the pursuit of success. In fact, they are embraced and honored for traits indicative of leadership.

The American is the most ideological of people. The committed Republican voter, for example, is often a Christian first, then an American, then a conservative, and then a Republican. Support for the major party is therefore hardly automatic.

The elected representative of the American people is largely answerable to a seemingly omnipotent and uncompromising ideological movement, not a centralized bureaucratic office of a party. Indeed Americans harbor a degree of suspicion in relation to the elites of the political party, including the silver-haired and silver-tongued politician of too many years— a result of the political party's dilution of principle, bastard-ization of ideas, and culture of compromise. Conservative Americans understand far better than their counterparts in the outside world that the Left preaches "civility" in their effort to silence criticism, and they seek to disparage the detractor, as ignorant or extreme. In matters of the national interest, silence is not golden; it's yellow.

The negotiation and settlement of political differences appears to be scarcest in the contemporary times of this nation. People here pick a side; the middle is not an accept-able location. Passion is such that it is rare to find a husband and wife where one is Republican and the other Democratic. The American father frowns on his daughter dating a man of different political persuasion or belonging to a family of such disposition. Politics is culture. Such considerations appear far earlier in the line of questioning of the parent than they would in outsider nations. These matters deepen the political chasm, encouraging cultural and political homogeneity. It is why America is so divided now.

Political office holds little charm for many people here as it often comes at a great price: a loss of conscience and self-respect. Americans can live with the prospect of being ostracized, should the alternative be to submit, or conform. Better to go down in flames for what you believe in than just towing the line. For all the commitment to the principles of a good, constitutionally limited government, conservative Americans must always remember that strong and effective government can and has enhanced the nation of America.

Conservative Americans have been the architect of the American dream, and great governance has played its role in ensuring the American formula remains intact. Americans have been assured until now in that their country, unlike others, has advanced human liberty. Citizens here understand the role of their state in eliminating polio in their children with vaccines and protecting the great wilderness areas of Yellowstone and Yosemite with national parks. This is, without question, the most libertarian land of them all, but it is a natural component of the American people, not of their ideology. Americans may be more disposed to the libertarian streak than any other people, but they must be careful, for any journey to the land of the libertarian and its territories of anarchy will surely be the last.

Few can disagree that America could do with a strong dose of libertarian sentiment right now. But while it may be the fashion of the day, it must be remembered that at their heart, activist libertarians are pro-pot, pro-porn, and pro-pacifism, and these are not representative of the cultural values of America, nor are they in the spirit of its founding. It's not the libertarians' spirit that is the problem; it's their cultural presence. I believe God underwrites not undermines the individual American's freedom.

9

Tradition

Visiting outsiders who immerse themselves in American culture can swiftly deduce that the strength of this land lies in her celebration of individuality. I find that this celebration accounts for the incomparable diversity of the American population and the extremities that exist. Diversity is influenced by any number of variables, including geography and demography, but diversity defines the nation and prompts many to hold the same position as the American historian and definer of modern liberalism in this country, Henry Steele Commager, when he said, "Every effort to confine Americanism to a single pattern, to constrain it to a single formula, is disloyalty to everything that is valid in Americanism." But that's relativist drivel. The truth is there is a quintessential American.

The great freedom of the American people has given them one of the most powerful senses of free will. Every nation has both a history and a spirit, and Americans have perhaps the grandest of each. Character belongs not just to the individual but to the country.

Americans who best represent this nation are those who believe that God is the source of their blessings and opportunities, unlike the outsider with his feeble glances at his government to offer him mere shadows of opportunities. Humanity will always produce the sin of hypocrisy, but exceptions do not disprove the general rule. This nation is not without the ills plaguing other nations at this time, but these ills have only had limited effect on the national culture. Americans enjoy a lifestyle that is the fruit of determination, hard work, and right choices.

During my visits here, I've witnessed strands of thought and aggressively held values: gratitude, optimism, pride, and spirituality rate highly among them. The character of the conservative American people is an intricately sewn quilt, a patchwork in many ways. Their faith, which they wear on their sleeves, molds them. Their attitude is guided by the Constitution, not a stipulation of the power of the government, but an outline of citizens' rights. It restrains their government, not them. But most outstanding is their faithful appreciation of the simple matters of life, like faith and family—matters of permanence and significance. The priorities in a country the size of America vary, as they do even within the course of the individual life. But deep in the areas of the "real America," the priorities within these populations have undergone scant change, and there's a very good probability that in fifty years, little will have changed. More so than anywhere else, the chronological bigotry that lies at the heart of the Left is rejected.

There is still the homecoming tradition to welcome back alumni or former residents on a sunny Friday afternoon, where residential streets are lined with people sitting on their lawns, and parades are full of young children riding tricycles adorned with American flags. There's still a devotion to church organization. The comforts of life are prized here; Americans may work harder than the outsider, but whatever free time they have, they enjoy deeply. These images of natural, normal, healthy community life, often associated with the past promote little change.

While many elites of the outside world, and the few who reside in pockets of this nation, have drowned their minds in the waves of the swelling sea of secularism, conservative Americans understand the civic consequences of their religion; they recognize its role in fostering good citizenship. Foreigners cannot help but be impressed by the level of activity of the American in civic life. Outsiders feel that, while they may breathe, they merely exist in their own nation; their energy is quashed, their creativity is squelched, and their ambition is lifeless. Such is the nature of outsider countries, whose cultural nose immediately guides it to the addictive smells of the insatiable government, whatever its predicament. But in this grand nation, the same outsiders are exhilarated and emancipated, swept away by the winds of opportunity. Titillating and arresting, this true liberty is an intoxicating drink that nourishes the soul and celebrates individual talent.

Americans find great joy in their spouses and children. To observe the American family is at once endearing and inspirational; it is, at least on the surface, the most idealized familial image. I cannot help but feel that the family is at its most natural and greatest in this nation. The man here is the most child-oriented of men, his lifestyle shaped around his children. Weekends are spent playing with them. Bookshelves are lined with pictures and accomplishments. And parents are proud of the smallest and newest bit of knowledge their children have learned and are eager to share it with family and friends.

At age eighteen, Americans almost invariably begin their individual journeys of independence, a baby eagle pushed out of its nest by its mother, reluctantly but for its own good. The adult eagle wants to see if her child can fly; she understands that life and flight are in the struggle, and that, without struggle, there can be no growth. I wonder if this is a remnant of the great frontier age of this nation, when a boy became a man by leaving civilization, or at least the comfort of his parents, and blazing a new trail for himself.

In comparison, many other nations nest their children for a much longer time, often refusing to allow their young to grow. In those cultures, they wish for young men and women to extend their adolescence for as long as they can. The entitlement state is an indispensable assistance to this aim. Youth is prized in the welfare state with people in their sixties dressing as they may have in their twenties. The striking irony of this is that the self-appointed intellectual guardians—media, academia and the Left in general—are also trying to turn adults into infants. That is called the nanny state.

It is perhaps this shorter time span at home for Americans that translates into a greater emphasis on their children; parents effectively have only eighteen years to shape them before their children's presence becomes part-time. Americans always find a reason or season to celebrate with the family and friends of their community. Christmas, Easter and Thanksgiving, as well as Graduation, Father's Day, Memorial Day, Labor Day, and Mother's Day are major events in the American calendar.

While Americans are a people of enormous comfort and are engineers of their world, they don't easily fall prey to complacency. Indeed, they are always prepared and flexible to deal with life's challenges. They are not likely to collapse into hysterical laughter, but they certainly enjoy humor. A casual bunch, they revert to using first names quickly, in the absence of exceptional circumstances. While it may vary somewhat depending on region, I find Americans to be most polite. And I seldom encounter an older American who is unhappy with where they live. More often than not, they are likely to say they would not live elsewhere.

Conservative Americans are a most thankful people, glad to be alive, a condition helped in no small way by their religion. Gratitude is the guard against the engines of envy and greed, and Americans live and give with open hands and hearts. They adhere to the wisdom of the ancient writers of the book of Proverbs: "Do not withhold good from those who deserve it when it is in your power to act" (Pro 3:27).

Americans are robust and proficient, investing in meaningful work and deep relationships. And you can't bypass their optimistic character. They are the type of people who feel that if there is a will, there is a way; this, compared to the more likely completion of the phrase by others, *where there is a will, I want to be in it.* Cowards are never in it. But winners never quit.

Patriotic Americans are always prepared to help their country to overcome a national challenge or problem, regardless of their own abilities. While emotional, they are almost always pragmatic. This is in line with Tocqueville's assessment: "A thousand special causes have singularly concurred to fix the mind of the American upon purely practical objects. His passions, his wants, his education, and everything about him seem to unite in drawing the native of the United States earthward."[1]

Americans are often demonized for their pride, and no dispute can exist about that: they are proud individuals. But Americans have a valid reason for their pride. They are not interested in trumpeting false claims to greatness; rather, Americans realize that their cultural and individual achievements are worthy of praise. This is a reality in which they revel. This recognition of true achievement propels them forward. After all, the virtue of humility is not to deny one's own talents or gifts, but to be respective and deferential. Humility can influence others and exercising your talents and gifts for the good of others is commendable. But let's be honest: an America without swagger is no America at all.

Younger Americans are transient people who uproot themselves regularly, more so than people of any other nation. They are likely to have moved within the last decade at least twice, often well beyond the borders of their counties or states. Their transience is not a matter of instability; these actions merely reflect the irresistible lust for the fresh adventure, their preparedness to take on risk, and their perpetual pursuit of the American dream. To observers, there is seldom a minute in the lives of Americans that their subconscious minds are not dedicated to their right to pursue happiness.

Exposed to the geographical diversity of this land, outsiders find different exceptionalism in each of the states. But in my observation, the mammoth state of Texas stands alone. Texas is more than a state of mind and area; it is almost a nation.

The land of Texas is enough to excite any true-blooded conservative American. The Texan is the most American of the Americans; fearsome folks irrespective of physical size, they walk with unmistakable moxie and possess an unfailing courtesy. They require no words to make their displeasure clear; one needs only cast a cursory glance into their eyes. Texans are people of tradition, family, strength, hospitality, generosity, self-reliance, patriotism, and God. They are fortresses of common sense, directness, and traditional values. *Texas is to America what America is to the world. Indispensable.*

Texans have a merciless contempt for political correctness, and a steadfast refusal to embrace the new emasculated and morally debased world. This makes it truly a piece of living history, one of the only places left where traditional values, Christianity, patriotism, and common sense still prevail. Not to mention, the moxie, swagger, and bravado of Texas are intoxicating. I love it. *With the current trends of the world, it is any right-thinking person's retirement plan.* It would appear that the stories of the Texan are all true; there is almost nothing a Texan cannot do. Even if outnumbered and outgunned, the Texan is never out of the fight. Of the state's fifteen major rivers, not one is a river of negativity. Conservative Texans surround themselves in faith, with even a monument of the Ten Commandments on the grounds of their state capitol, and they understand that they cannot soar with the eagles if they peck with the chickens. Their state is a frontier, a lamp unto the feet of the American people, and a light unto their path. If you were ever to require guidance, the Texan, I feel, should be your first contact. *If you weren't born there, get there as quick as you can.*

It is hard for the outsider to imagine that a society such as the Texan's exists; it very difficult for me to conceive of a finer human society. The inspiring words of the heroic Navy SEAL, and a model of strength and virtue hailing from East Texas, Marcus Luttrell, are instructive for the embattled American:

> Most of all, I'm an American. And when the bell sounds, I will come out fighting for my country and for my teammates. If necessary, to the death.
>
> And that's not just because the SEALs have trained me to do so; it's because I'm willing to do so. I'm a patriot, and I fight with the Lone Star of Texas on my right arm and another Texas flag over my heart. For me, defeat is unthinkable.[2]

The presence of the South Carolinian in the southeast of this nation is another example of exceptionalism. Utterly individualistic, the South Carolinian lives in a society defined by the power of the state, not the federal government. They, second only to the Texan, value the individual and the individual state above all else, including the federal government. It was the state of South Carolina to first declare war on the federal government in 1861, waiting just four days after the election of Lincoln to begin the process. The same fiery conviction that the state, not the federal government, should run the state, has not changed in the last century and a half. South Carolina remains one of only two states in the union to sponsor its own military academy. This is not only a relic of the statist fervor felt before the outbreak of the American Civil War but also a powerful symbol today of state superiority over federal jurisdiction. I had great pleasure speaking at the Citadel, the Military College of South Carolina, in Charleston.

South Carolinians are a people defined by tradition but molded by modernity, a people who affirm their past but, more important, affirm their future. *God bless the Palmetto State.* Both South Carolinians and Texans have a life that is authentically theirs.

***

It would appear that even the nonreligious men and women of this nation welcome the influence of God, if only in the abstract. Even secular Americans often unwittingly speak the vocabulary of faith and its consequent optimism. This is testimony to the powerful and permanent influence religion has had in this national culture. Underpinning the secularists' utterances are their actions. The three columns of optimism, faith, and individuality provide the high-pitched roof of abundance, size, and continual increase. Americans appear to follow the words of Genesis more closely than any other people: "God blessed them, saying: Be fruitful and multiply, and fill the earth, and subdue it; and rule over the fish of the sea and over the birds of the sky and over every living thing that moves on the earth." (Gen. 1:28). This is a possible explanation of why the American thinks and acts on a grander scale than his counterparts in other nations when it comes to the size of his roads, his vehicles, his meal portions, and his visions for the future. The "go for it" approach of Americans is at odds with that of people who are close-fisted, environmentally sensitive, and insecure about the future.

Historically, the American male exudes masculinity, and the female has radiated equivalent femininity. The man here still tends to cherish his man-cave, that space of reverential silence in the family home dedicated to male pursuits and interests. To visitors coming here from other Western countries, familiar with the destructive blending of gender roles in their own and neighboring nations, the comparative distinction and preservation of nature and tradition are refreshing. Unfortunately, recent times have witnessed all Western nations, including America, to be subject to the emasculation of society, which has weakened the traditional male to the point where he feels uncomfortable. Men can't do what they used to do because they are afraid. The feminist elites, and others, who want to do harm to men now have the systems in place and the culture on their side to do it. Not to mention the weasel words like "bully" and "harassment." It's even reached the point where men often feel uncomfortable even approaching women to make an introduction. And you can forget flirting—dangerous!

Men should be men, and women should be women.

The Creator of the universe has ordered things to work a certain way. America must uphold the male-female distinction for it is critical to civilization. Men are to be the leaders and the head of their families, not in a domineering way but in a strong gentle manner that imbues a sense of stability and security. When you force a change on the natural roles and disrupt the order of society, it brings chaos and destruction. Feminism has done nothing but tear the family apart and emasculate men. There is no celebration of the feminine in feminism. There are significant dangers: The deliberate relegation of American male pastimes such as going to the range, watching sports, hanging out with your buddies or smoking cigars—has led to men in America being alienated and, on occasion, isolated in society. The continued efforts to decimate men and male culture by removing their confidence and creating hysteria around sexual harassment, have been gaining traction. This indicates that America, like Europe, is embracing Left-wing feminist ideology, which is deeply disturbing. America's national conversation needs to be careful not to descend any more than it already has into sissy language, and an attack on masculinity.

Tocqueville critiqued the objectives of feminism long before its destructive second wave, and he noted the American exceptionalism:

> There are people in Europe who, confounding together the different characteristics of the sexes, would make man and woman into beings not only equal but alike. They would give to both the same functions, impose on both the same duties, and grant to both the same rights;

they would mix them in all things—their occupations, their pleasures, their business. It may readily be conceived that by thus attempting to make one sex equal to the other, both are degraded, and from so preposterous a medley of the works of nature nothing could ever result but weak men and disorderly women.[3]

These matters and portrayal of gender are of limited revelation; they are entirely consistent with the famous characters of the literature and film in America. The American lady is exceptional in her dedication to family and to organization in the important matters of church, community, charity, and politics. Driven more by her values than perhaps some of her outsider counterparts, she is the rock of her family and, in times of crisis, her community and nation. She is often the keeper of the family calendar. In the veins of each American female courses the blood of the famous cultural icon Rosie the Riveter. The American female is most certainly equal to the American man as the outsider female is to her male equivalent; she simply embraces her differences with joy.

Armed

L et me begin with this. This is an excerpt of a speech I gave as the keynote speaker at the Centenary Celebration of the Arizona State Rifle and Pistol Association in Phoenix in June 2012:

I want to speak to the Second Amendment. I want to speak about the right to bear arms. Because there is no criticism of America more widespread, more vociferous, more universal than the Second Amendment right of the American citizen.

Ladies and gentlemen, I belong to a generation of Australians that have never picked up a gun. When I was just eleven years old, the federal government implemented gun reform in the wake of a dreadful and heart-wrenching massacre conducted by an insane man brandishing an AR-15. The government of the day implemented a comprehensive and elaborate gun buy-back scheme where Australians, the compliant people that we are, visited our local police stations and handed in our firearms.

In doing this, the government, while well-intentioned, took the guns out of the hands of the law-abiding citizen, leaving only the criminals armed.

In the sixteen years since this reform, there has been negligible change to the crime rate, other than a spike in knife activity and violent assault.

Any advocate of gun ownership is considered extreme and dangerous. The Daisy Red Ryder BB gun that my father played with as a child, and which sat under many an Australian Christmas tree for generations, is outlawed unless you have a special permit, safe, serial, and code stamp.

I know this. I spoke to the Daisy factory staff in Rogers, Arkansas, one tour, and as a gift, they allowed me to construct my own Red Ryder, which they sent to me. They had even disabled the toy—it could not shoot a pellet. I received a letter from Australian Customs and Immigration, and the first line read: "Dear Mr. Adams, we are in possession of an illegal firearm addressed to you." It went on to explain what I would require to have the gun released to me. I would need police clearance, a gun license, a three-day safety course, a safe, a serial code number stamped on it by a gunsmith, and the gun would need to be registered to a gun shop. When I suggested it would only be a wall piece, the bureaucrat I spoke to almost went into meltdown, informing me I could hold up a bank with that gun.

That is the state of play in Australia, your fellow frontier nation.

Now, I want every person in this room to listen really carefully to what I am about to say, because I could be living your future if you do not remain vigilant. Nothing, ladies and gentlemen, nothing is more emblematic of the exceptionalism of America than the Second Amendment. Without the Second Amendment, there are no other amendments: the rest of the Constitution is a recommendation. It defines what America is about. It speaks to the character of America and to the mentality and philosophy of the American. It reflects why America came into being and the success of its human experiment. Civilian disarmament is based on the assumption that people are irresponsible (unless they work for the government). America was founded on the opposite premise.

Just as there is no greater moral imperative than keeping America strong, there is no greater moral imperative than supporting and advocating the constitutional right to bear arms. You take away the guns of America, you take away America.

Let's set the record straight here. Because I'm done with the elites and their misinformation. I'm done with the namby-pamby society. I'm done with the effete urbanites. I'm done with the world-citizen politicians. They have fired thousands of volleys of shots, wielding their weapon of distortion in their war on individual liberty, and the casualties have been truth and reality.

The right to bear arms is not wrong, immoral, evil, bad, or unnecessary. It's the opposite. The right to bear arms is the greatest test of genuine freedom, the best protection of you, your family, and your property; the greatest deterrent of governmental overreach, the greatest disincentive to foreign invasion, the greatest defense to the two cancers threatening the West—radical Islam and socialism—and the greatest asset to a confident and individualistic society.

If you don't understand why owning a gun is important or necessary, you don't get freedom. If you don't get that criminals will always have guns, then you don't get logic. If it does not concern you that the very first act of virtually every totalitarian regime over the last hundred years has been to disarm its population, then you are beyond help. If you want to greet a home invader, carjacker, thief, or rapist with an umbrella and harsh words, give up your rights.

Ladies and gentlemen, it is time to replant and reinforce the spirit of individualism, self-reliance, and independence in all areas that made this nation great.

Americans face vicious criticism of their right to keep and bear arms as enshrined in the Second Amendment of their magnificent Constitution. This nation has a deep history and respect of the military. Outsiders, destitute of liberty and armed by their socialistic masters with collectivist and politically correct proclivities from a young age, point accusingly at the gun culture of this country as evidence of their own moral and cultural superiority over the American. But they are wrong.

The controls on firearms by the governments of the outside world are further tactics in their continued emasculation operation. In the Western world, except in America, the gun is allowed no role in life. The gun owner or advocate in these cultures is considered the most uncouth and offensive of citizens. In my home country, it's bad optics to even be photographed with a gun, particularly if you're a government official or hold elected office. Yet a society in which the criminal is armed and the law-abiding citizen is unarmed can never be a free society. Why would you want to give criminals any advantage over the law-abiding citizens anyway? This reality was presciently explained by eighteenth-century Italian politician Cesare Beccaria:

> Laws that forbid the carrying of arms . . . disarm only those who are neither inclined nor determined to commit crimes. . . . Such laws make things worse for the assaulted and better for the assailants; they serve rather to encourage than to prevent homicides, for an unarmed man may be attacked with greater confidence than an armed man.[1]

Many of the most zealous advocates of gun control have also been advocates of leniency toward criminals. This is an irony that should not be lost.

The American is cognizant that the first act of every totalitarian regime of the last century was the disarmament of the regular citizenry. An unarmed population will lose any contest between it and the government. As the saying goes, "The strongest reason for people to retain the right to keep and bear arms is, as a last resort, to protect themselves against tyranny in government."

This is embossed in the psyche of Americans and their culture. It is because of these fears that the famed spirited vigilance in the preservation of their Second Amendment rights exists in these people. The disarmament of the civilian is premised on the irresponsibility and distrust of the citizen. And it is in opposition to the premise of the founding of the

American nation: an inclination to suspect the government, not the people. Herein lies the fundamental difference.

The right to bear arms is a centerpiece of the American's exceptionalism; it's synonymous with freedom. The flag of freedom flies with a permanent gust of wind blown by the Second Amendment. Here it is a most true assertion that a citizen without a gun is a captain without a ship. This fundamental right has been under steady fire from elites, who have armed the sheep of their nations with the ammunition of falsehood. Outsiders believe that the firearm is unnecessary, a tool of the bad for much evil. In most countries, citizens consider that government control or restrictions of the firearm are not only rightful, but necessary. But the truth about the firearm has been majorly distorted in the non-American society. The reality is that the right to bear arms is the greatest test of the genuineness of freedom, and the best protection of oneself, one's family, and one's property. It is the greatest deterrent to governmental overreach, the greatest disincentive against foreign invasion, and the greatest asset to a confident and individualistic society. Of course, this is crazy talk anywhere outside of America. Isn't it amazing that the rest of the world is prepared to marvel at American brilliance and innovation, and to acknowledge that it is the most advanced country in the world, but it is not prepared to consider the merits of their Second Amendment? Or consider its role in their success?

It often feels as if Americans have a sufficient number of weapons to arm the entire population twice over. There is absolutely no way this nation will ever be overcome by means of physical invasion, as purportedly enunciated by the commander-in-chief of the Imperial Japanese Navy during the Second World War, Isoroku Yamamoto: "You cannot invade the mainland United States. There would be a rifle behind every blade of grass." The right of the American to bear arms ensures the restraint of the federal government, and this right floods the veins of international enemies with fear. If every country provided an equivalent right to bear arms, it would similarly restrain government and protect them from their international enemies.

The women of the American nation are as likely as men, if not more so, to keep and bear firearms and to provide the greatest advocacy for the Second Amendment. In the quintessential American business spirit, the gun has become almost a fashion accessory, designed for the woman's use with detailed decorative color and flair. The American child is most likely to own a Daisy Red Ryder or a similar toy, considered an illegal firearm by the outsiders' nations. The elderly American is empowered, as the female American is, by the firearm. It is ironic that those who claim there is a war on women do not support a female's opportunity to defend herself.

Americans believe in the right of the individual to self-defense and the capability to protect oneself, one's family, and one's property. It is true that the American may have more sympathy for the vigilante than the outsider, although the outsider often wrongly considers mere self-defense tantamount to vigilantism. It's sad that some people have such a low opinion of themselves. *You need a gun, a whip, and a chair to deal with an American. Such is the American spirit.*

The preservation of individual liberty is at the forefront of the American mind-set. Great numbers of American citizens would readily explain that, upon the election of the last president, they immediately went to their gun stores to purchase more weaponry and ammunition because they knew attacks on the Second Amendment were imminent. This indication of the nature of the American people and the lengths they travel to protect the freedom and liberty so vigorously fought for by their forefathers leaves little doubt: Americans are truly exceptional beings—an uncommon people with an uncommon cause in a very common world. And they should be weary of backdoor gun control—the control of ammunition. *What good is your gun without ammo?*

Imperiled Future

Americans are unsettled; their famed optimism is on the wane. They are sharply cognizant that the world considers this to be the Chinese century, part of the overall global consensus that the finest days of the American nation are a matter of history. But don't be buffaloed by "experts." The best is yet to come.

While Americans may not compare themselves to the outsider, they nevertheless involuntarily sense the nation has gone awry. But this is most unfamiliar terrain for Americans, a people accustomed to charting only the most exceptional of waters from birth. They struggle to remember a time when their beloved country was not the lion in the world zoo. Despite their recent great unease, insecurity, and economic ache, American minds should disbelieve that their greatest fears will materialize. *Despair is not only unattractive; it's un-American.*

In days past, the mere mention of the American economy has always instantly puffed the chests of Americans with pride, but today it drains the color from their faces. The unprecedented magnitude of their national debt is a source of immense distress for many. Almost $6 trillion of the debt held by the public is owned by foreign investors. (To put that into perspective, if you'd started a business the day Jesus was born and lost a million dollars every year, you'd be in better financial shape than the American government.) A public and private debt burden totaling almost four times the value of the gross domestic product is unsustainable and perilous. It affects everything. America should not have a message of debt; it should have a message of life.

The government's power to control an individual's life derives from its power to tax. And while it is true that all manner of people submit their tax money reluctantly, Americans are the most ill disposed of all to taxation. A new tax triggers immediate disquiet between the American and the governmental authority responsible for it. While it is grudgingly accepted, it will be continually questioned. This is unlike the "go along, get along" crowd in other Western nations, where such moves are met with limited or hushed opposition.

With any nation, the nucleus of national power rests with the economy; a battered economy is a strained power, always wrestling. But much like her story, America's economy is exceptional, for it is undergirded by two mighty forces: military power and technological advantage. The overwhelming financial debt of the American people that has them wiping the sweat off their brows does not inhibit their key capability: to be the driving influence on global markets. No matter how bad the debt is, America will continue to be the driving influence on global markets. The world's perceptions of America being able to meet its obligations, and its ability to print the world's premiere reserve currency, largely makes the national debt merely a number. The only way perceptions will alter is if the debt becomes unserviceable, which would decimate the economy.

It must be said that Americans have a boomerang nature. They are a resilient population committed not just to survival but also to the preservation of exceptionalism. This phenomenon was first identified by the genius of the twenty-seven-year-old Tocqueville with his pithy illumination: "The greatness of America lies not in being more enlightened than any other nation, but rather in her ability to repair her faults." Although Americans have endured dreary leadership on the home front, hostile aggression abroad, and the roughest of economic times, neither recession nor depression nor the demands of war on multiple occasions has more than temporarily disoriented and hindered them. They are much like the American invention Kevlar—five times stronger than steel.

Winston Churchill described socialism as the "philosophy of failure, the creed of ignorance, and the gospel of envy."[1] Failure, ignorance, and envy starkly oppose and disrupt the life and culture of America. These conditions wilt the personality and constrain the heart. Their absence means that the American is most unversed in socialism; bureaucrats, leftists, collectivists, statists, and progressives are the axis of the enemies of America. The Left will always seek to cause some Americans to be fearful, resentful, and hostile toward other Americans; it's how they roll and how they win elections.

Outsiders are swift to foretell the advance of the Chinese. It is ironic that perhaps the greatest advice for the American of today comes from the Chinese symbol for the word *crisis*, comprising two words: *danger* and *opportunity*. Opportunity rarely arrives without danger, and the American people are more capable than any others to defeat their threats and emerge, as they have in previous dangers, stronger than ever. They must return each inch of their land to opportunities for the innovator or entrepreneur, to replicate what Cape Canaveral in the state of Florida did for the space program. They need only focus on themselves; the great Chinese bully will suffer the same fate as those nations before him. He may threaten economically and geopolitically at this time, but no nation can sustain success without granting its citizens economic and political liberty. The Chinese, with all their money, will always be the poor man's America.

China's denial of liberty will always render it but a bootlace on the American shoe. Also, less than 5 percent of the Chinese have God as an important feature of their lives. It will only be when Bibles and churches appear in overwhelming numbers in China that the American may have a genuine competitor. *You won't be asked, "Do you want fries with that Coke?" in Mandarin anytime soon.*

It may well be true that China is currently exhibiting the traditional drive and pride of the American to some degree, and its growing economic prowess is indisputable. Even in the best case scenario, China has a long journey to superpower status. There are social, political, and demographic hurdles such as a gender imbalance, growing political awareness of the middle class, and increasing social tensions. American technology will prove to be painful to Chinese leadership ambitions.

Americans, in dealing with the avalanche of predictions about the ascent of China, must not lose perspective. They should remember the false claims of the inevitability of the rise of the Japanese economy a quarter of a century ago, and the fate of many other communist nations. US leadership is vindicated by the emergence of a global and middle class in India and China.

America must not let its regrets and dreads steal its energy to succeed today. When the game is on the line, winners always want the ball.

An Almost Treasonous Culture War

Imagine if Ronald Reagan had followed the dictates of moral relativism. Where would the world be now? The dangers for the American include the malignant cancer of political correctness: government overreach that seeks to replicate a European system of social democracy; the transformation of the classroom to the desires of bureaucratic elites; and cultural relativism with the warm embrace of the West's failed multiculturalism. Political correctness encompasses the objectively and intrinsically sinful acts of abortion and homosexual marriage, and the rise of Islam in the context of world history. I feel that Americans must be both priestly and prophetic, keeping their eyes on the failures of other nations of the world to save themselves from the errors of their fellow humans. They must observe the demography of the European and reject what perhaps first began with President Roosevelt: an ambition for a different America, with public institutions that the great Alexis de Tocqueville would today find unrecognizable and of eminent disappointment.

Significant cultural change is neither instant nor achieved in one deft move; such change is only ever achieved gradually. The people of the other nations of the world were not always infected with the steady erosion of values that besiege them today. Instead, like an unwary frog in a pot, they were slowly boiled to death. Had they been aware of their potential fate, the Europeans, the Australians, the Canadians, and the Brits would almost certainly have refused to begin the process. *Trust me on that.*

It is difficult to judge if Americans, with their famed resistance, are still outside the cooking pot of the secular elite or whether they have already jumped into the pot and the heat is being slowly applied. Such judgment is difficult because, once more, it is a case of the American people falling below their *own* potential, not that of any other nation. Americans, in either scenario, have benefited from the historical experience of others and have the clearest course before them: not to enter the pot, or if it's too late for that, to jump out immediately. When it comes to the kitchen, America just needs to go back to the original recipe.

The secular elite are by no means the pulse on the American wrist, but their growing and meddlesome efforts through the radio, television, newspaper, classroom, and lecture hall, do capture Americans' ears. These elites wish to perform dramatic surgery on the American heart that would render the nation unrecognizable. The ever-creeping, well-worn, and familiar catalog of clichés, accompanied by the concealing burka of political correctness, reminds visitors of their own nations. These political and cultural elites, motivated by a fraudulent secular moral superiority, paint America deceitfully, using not one lick of red, white, and blue. *They should get right or get out.*

The American must instead listen to wiser voices, like that of the famous Roman philosopher and orator Cicero:

> A nation can survive its fools, and even the ambitious. But it cannot survive treason from within. An enemy at the gates is less formidable, for he is known and carries his banner openly. But the traitor moves amongst those within the gate freely, his sly whispers rustling through all the alleys, heard in the very halls of government itself. For the traitor appears not a traitor; he speaks in accents familiar to his victims, and he wears their face and their arguments, he appeals to the baseness that lies deep in the hearts of all men. He rots the soul of a nation, he works secretly and unknown in the night to undermine the pillars of the city, he infects the body politic so that it can no longer resist. A murderer is less to fear.

Americans must wage the most decimating of battles against the malady of political correctness; it greatly threatens the American people and their objectives, in both the homeland and internationally. *Say what you mean, mean what you say, and say it like it is.* In the creed of the politically correct, competition promotes inequality; Islam is a religion of peace; all cultures are of equal rank or value; wealth is a matter of guilt, save for the athlete or entertainer; the nation state is an outdated model; Christian, Western civilization is primarily accountable for poverty and all deficiencies in the world; and conditions of life are a matter of circumstance, not choice. What an absolute crock.

Race, gender, and class wars, the desired objectives of political correctness, are a tactic to divide a country. Their engine is the collection of professional offense-takers. Any buy-in leads to a populace that is a slave to "hurt feelings" and is paralyzed by tolerance.

The traditions of opportunity, freedom, hard work, and entrepreneurship are the building blocks of the culture and politics of America. These are not merely inimical to socialistic principles but also make this land a great conservative nation, the penultimate citadel of anti-socialism. This is why America elicits the hatred of the outsider who has been conditioned in collectivism and baptized in socialistic water. America is a conservative oasis in the world's socialist desert. For this reason, in the Leftist hierarchy of beliefs, anti-American autocracy is the trump card that beats gay rights, feminism, race, and freedom of speech (not that the Left ever really believed in that, anyway).

Americans must remember that cultural superiority is tangible matter, measured by objective scales. All human beings are equal, but not all cultures are equal. Ain't that the truth. No culture is without flaw, but some are better than others. Why should this country, the world's greatest, downwardly assimilate?

While any member of the elite class may howl in protest, such illogical socialistic rumination must fall on deaf ears. Even the castle of such rumination, the United Nations, uncharacteristically awards a Human Development Index ranking, using a series of measurements such as GDP per capita, literacy, life expectancy, women's rights, and strength of democracy. To insist that the Western culture, ensuring equality before the law and freedom of speech, is no different from the culture overseeing female genital mutilation, forced marriages, and honor killings, is most reprehensible. The cultural relativist is the husband of the bureaucratic internationalist; he desires the weakening of the nation state to create the body that governs for many. The bastard children of this illicit marriage are the edicts of multiculturalism and affirmative action, responsible for creating special-interest groups and incentivizing member-ship in them through a sense of empowerment that comes from those who benefit from the government help, while ushering in a new age of hostility. If Americans accept these groups, they will find that such groups will only assimilate in the form of understanding American weaknesses, and learning how to capitalize on them.

The nation that believes every culture is equal must expect new immigrants and new generations of previous immigrants to find little need for patriotism or loyalty. America: love it or leave it. *And let me preempt the accusations of racism for the hacks who dine out on race-baiting. The real racists are white liberals.*

The last thing a liberal wants is a color-blind society.

***

The elementary and secondary education system of America, formerly the most prized of the world, symbolized to the outsider by the yellow school bus, is today but a shadow of its former self. While not yet immediately visible to the outsider, statistical research utilizing various measures, along with the word of the older generation, insists the American child now lags in various educational measurements. It is not only the American suffering this predicament; it is widely and evenly spread throughout the West, but the opposite is true for the civilizations of the East.

Of particular uneasiness are the areas where deficiency is most pronounced: mathematics and science. The strategic survival of any nation depends on science, for science and security are inextricably linked. Americans need only look to their Israeli friends, people of similar scientific brilliance. The great threat to America and to the Western civilization that the United States has dominated is that America's scientific lead has been significantly closed. The American child is less likely than ever to pursue science in the latter years of secondary education or in college. The areas of mastery that are crucial to the future of the world, and essential for the challenges of the twenty-first century, will benefit the students who have the highest levels of mathematics, science, and creativity; this must once more become this land's focus.

These are not the only matters of concern that have the American sweating. The educators and industry representatives of the nation's schools espouse an altered, vacuous brand of Americanism. Academia is rife with secularism and anti-religious sentiment. Along with American exceptionalism in the burgeoning homeschooling experience, Americans must reclaim the classrooms of their children, too long the hostage of government intervention and union collaboration. The classroom of the average American school is today the tool of inculcation for the atheistic, politically correct, and self-flagellating collectivist. The American flag must remain more visible than the school mascot in the nation's schools. It should be suspended in every classroom, gymnasium, lobby, and office. The national anthem must continue to be sung at school assemblies and athletic events; these matters of patriotism are central to the greatness of the American nation and any exceptional educational experience. At a secondary level, Americans should mandate Constitution classes; elementary school should devote a full year to US geography, since pride accompanies prosperity.

Tocqueville said of American education, "Americans are taught from birth that they must overcome life's woes and impediments on their own. Social authority makes them mistrustful and anxious, and they rely upon its power only when they cannot do without it. This first becomes apparent in the schools, where children play by their own rules and punish infractions they define themselves."[1]

While the *literati* have fashioned the history of the English-speaking nations in the clothes of their own self-loathing, generations of young British, Australian, and American children leave the doors of their classrooms awash with guilt. The red pens of the elites have ensured that historical exploration now bears the label of genocide, a mere chapter of the broader, vile chronicle of exploitation and racism. The education bureaucrats of this nation urge that the founding principles of this nation be viewed with suspicion. They teach students to automatically assume American guilt. They foster self-loathing and pander to minorities. They're not teachers:

they're wardens, incarcerating minds. This misuse of schools to undermine one's own society is not something confined to the United States or even to our own time. *But America must stop it.* I also fear for this nation because God is increasingly no longer a consideration in its government or its classrooms. And yet Christian faith tells the success of this country. The more vibrant the religion, the greater the creativity. The unprecedented advances of this country, in all arenas, have been enabled by faith.

This revisionist history that wears on its wrist a black arm-band endangers future generations of Americans and English-speaking people, to whom the world's liberty will one day be bequeathed. The American child must be pushed to the limit; educational standards must always remain high, for nothing rates higher than college achievement. Schools and universities alike must be prescient in their educational curriculum content; they must always educate students for employment posts that do not yet exist. Such is the mark of the true leading nation. Americans must prepare the future generations.

To secure their freedom, Americans must address these matters with urgency, restoring honesty and pride to the curriculum and correcting the national narrative in the minds of their young. Americans will not have truly reclaimed their children's classrooms until

- the birthdays of Washington and Lincoln are again celebrated with their symbols of honesty: the cherry tree and the return of change to a customer in New Salem;

- Columbus and other explorers are presented as the courageous innovators that they were;

- the First Thanksgiving is taught as an event celebrating the friendship of Pilgrims and Indians, through reenactments and a meal;

- US Constitution classes are instituted and required in secondary schools;

- Benjamin Franklin, universally revered as he was, is once more espoused as the "universal man";

- the Boston Tea Party is revealed as a great and courageous event;

- the poem and story of The Midnight Ride of Paul Revere are included in lesson plans;

- the American Revolution is portrayed as the glorious event it truly was;

- John Adams and Thomas Jefferson are focused on as founding fathers and important presidents (followed later by Theodore Roosevelt);

- Lewis and Clark are taught as heroes of the Louisiana Purchase;

- Manifest Destiny is accepted as reality;

- the great inventors and their inventions, such as the steamboat, telegraph, steel plow, reaper, electric lightbulb, telephone, phonograph, and assembly line, are taught;

- men such as Norman Berlaug, the father of the Green Revolution, are recognized;

- the Civil War is taught as the great moral triumph;

- the trinity of constitutional amendments that ended slavery and provided equal American rights (thirteenth, fourteenth, and fifteenth), are commemorated;

- women's right to vote is celebrated as a natural progression of freedom;

- the role of America in advancing democracy, particularly in the Spanish-American War and both world wars, is acknowledged and revered;

- the work of Alexis de Tocqueville appears in secondary textbooks and is studied in depth in later years.

Today's students are the future entrepreneurs, inventors, and overall stewards of this nation and the world. Furthermore, American children and teenagers must be taught to refuse to place any limits on individual human potential or on the role of Western civilization. The Left understand that to control tomorrow, you just need to control the children of today.

Universities are no different. Conservatives are denied tenure, and the entire college system has been infiltrated. It is why the outsider finds so many conservative think tanks here. Cultural institutions, such as the entertainment media, schools, and the print media on the whole in the last forty years have had a stranglehold on universities, and this country is no exception. The mainstream American media chose sides long ago, and they only want to play unopposed. They revile objectivity. They carry the water for the Western/European socialist model while loathing conservative talk radio, the blogosphere, and one cable news station that objectively reports. Socialism has a record of failure so blatant only an intellectual could ignore it. An argument can already be made that America's decision makers and opinion makers have been stunted by the university-bred doctrine of moral equivalence. *A free marketplace of ideas is American; politically correct intolerance must remain foreign.*

This nation has led the democratization of the West, and it will be the young Americans of today who will be charged with the responsibility of preserving the greatness and superiority of the West over the Rest. They must study the foundational texts of this civilization: the King James Bible, Isaac Newton's *Principia*, John Locke's *Two Treatises of Government*, Adam Smith's *Moral Sentiments* and *Wealth of Nations*, Edmund Burke's *Reflections on the Revolution in France*, William Shakespeare's plays, and selected speeches of Abraham Lincoln, Winston Churchill, and William Wilberforce.

For proceeding generations to uphold American greatness, they must return to an education untainted by left-wing ideology. Of the real threats posed to America today, few can be ranked higher in priority than this. If the American people are to continue their leadership of not only their own nation but also of others, they must determine with finality that their children should neither be educated nor, more aptly, indoctrinated by those with only contempt for American tradition.

Bring back the stern disciplinarians, the old-school guys and gals who made the best teachers.

***

Sadly, but in accordance to humanity, the purity Americans aspire to is often unmatched in action. The increasing absence of Judeo-Christian values are a major reason America is in grave danger. This nation is not without its shame, its house a haven for the avowed abortionist, whose deed is tragically protected by the law. No conflict more bitterly divides the American than abortion. This land is also the home of the most valiant supporters of life, a paradox only possible in this nation. The conflict between two fundamental rights—the right to privacy and the right to life—that cannot coexist inevitably forces a clear choice, and Americans, as the stained pages of history reveal, have erred monstrously in their chosen path. *It's a baby, not a choice.*

It cannot be denied: there exists a fundamental right to exercise control over what occurs to one's body. But there exists also the right of the unborn child to live. Shouldn't a woman's womb be the safest place on earth? Americans must understand the fundamental right to life is their only unlimited right, ultimate and trumping in its nature. When this right is absent, so is liberty. Without life there can be no future life; without the right to pursue life, the famous United States Constitution is worthless. If ever a more pointed example exists of the vacuousness of moral relativism than the idea of every woman determining whether abortion is moral, I am yet to hear it.

The American people must conduct the deepest searches of their national and personal conscience, realizing the inescapable fact that abortion is antithetical to their nation in that it denies the dreams of the unborn. Americans must conceive the truth: their destiny cannot be fulfilled until they give voice to those who could not, cannot, and will not be able to vote or speak unless they are allowed to live. Innocent life must be cherished. Without it, innocence is lost in all respects. It's time to end the war on life.

Similarly, this land bears in very small parts an almost homosexual and secular fascism, intent on redefining the greatest and most fundamental institution of civilization: marriage. While traditional marriage is protected in a handful of states, many have successfully redefined the institution to permit gay marriage—a definition that removes the very need for the institution and is contrary to the moral character of this nation and the heterosexual ideal of the Bible. Sadly some Americans have forgotten that the sole reason for this institution, in principle, was the social regulation of the obligations associated with procreation. This is not to suggest those marriages of man and woman incidentally unable to conceive due to age or infertility are irrelevant; by standard definition, they are included. But marriage between two of the same sex is, in principle, impossible because it is redefining the institution to the point of removing the need. These are matters that the American people must deal with for their full potential to be realized. Gay marriage is less about "marriage equality" and more about extinguishing the male-female distinction, a biological fact and anthropological truth indispensable to life. Marriage is the fundamental building block of all human civilization. No one is entitled to redefine a foundational institution of civil society that has existed for millennia.

Does this nation have a character problem? It does, although not as much as any other country. But is it enough to be the smartest kid in a dumb class? To respond to militant secularism and antifamily in the postmodern West, Americans must unite pro-family organizations, scholars, legislators, and activists seeking to restore the natural family as the fundamental social unit.

Political correctness means we allow ourselves to be bullied by the anti-bullying crusade.

It may sound strange, but despite the amount of immorality in America, it's still the most virtuous country in the world. And despite the clear decline in American character, I still observe a unique, deep obligation among patriotic Americans for their country to be "good" and live up to the expectations of their national self-image.

Radical Islam

For almost fourteen hundred years, Islamists have sought and fought to conquer other civilizations. Events lining the pages of history prove it. Since the seventh century, at least. From battle to battle, generation to generation, it has never stopped. And it never will. Multiculturalism and *Al-Hijra*, the Islamic doctrine of immigration, have been the tools to promote Islam. There have been some eighteen thousand deadly terror attacks committed in the name of Allah in the last ten years. Here, America must heed the example of Europe.

The religion of Islam, when obeyed inflexibly, literally, and with an adherence to strictures, is a perpetual act of vandalism visited upon the ideals of the Western world, and one that will ultimately threaten America's existence. It is an evil, failed and wrong ideology. It's as simple as that. Muslims' own "holy book" mandates that they kill every man, woman, or infant who is a non-Muslim. "They desire that you should disbelieve as they have disbelieved, so that you might be (all) alike; therefore take not from among them (the unbelievers) friends until they flee (their homes) in Allah's way; but if they turn back, then seize them and kill them wherever you find them, and take not from among them a friend or a helper." (Sura 4, verse 89). If they truly follow their own "scriptures," they're obligated to kill every American, Canadian, Belgian, Australian, etc.—who is not a Muslim. Islam further teaches that non-Muslims are less than fully human, that they are "dirty," "feces," and so forth.

The qualities deceptively attributed to the religion of Islam, most notably the ambition of peace, by the politically correct outsider are outrageous and entirely misplaced. It is the modern Western world, a beacon powered by America and its fellow English-tongued cousins across the oceans, that have sought peace.

Islam opposes everything Western, all the way down to thinking that if there is a woman in a bikini on a beach, she deserves to be raped-"free meat" as Australian Sheik Taj Din El- Hilaly once said.[1] In Europe and Australia, many Muslim immigrants have not only rejected Western moral and social values but have also become more fanatical since arriving.

All theology is political; it has a bearing on the events of the process of politics. America must jettison the urging for diplomacy with radical Islam. Americans should note the events on the pages of history when dealing with the struggle against the radical Islamist of either overt or stealth form. From the seventh century, Islamists have scrapped with individuals, religions, or nations different from themselves, from the Battle of Tours in 732 to the siege of Constantinople in 1453 to the Battle of Lepanto in 1571 to the Battle of Vienna in 1683. Since its inception, Islam has gone to war, not because it was threatened, but to conquer and convert people, to bring mankind to Islam.

The Islamists of today are not representative of a distorted Islam, as the secular elites may proclaim; to the contrary, they clearly follow the teachings of the Koran, within which lie the Hadith and the Sura. In order to assess and decide their future actions, Americans should familiarize themselves with the teachings of the Wahhabism developed in the eighteenth century and the workings of the leaders of the Muslim Brotherhood.

America should never be at war with a nameless enemy, and yet due to fear and political correctness, it often is. For their own survival, Americans should consider the stillborn supposition of the elite outsider—that no words critical of the Islamic faith must be uttered, for fear of inciting hatred—to be irrelevant. They must instead, for the continued health and unity of this nation, deafeningly and without a hint of hesitation, roar their opinion.

Americans must reject the cultural, political, and intellectual bully that is the radical Islamist of stealth persuasion. Surreptitious Muslims are using our tolerance to play us like a harp, ensuring restless sleep for both America and its friends. Some American Muslims are beginning to exhibit the behavior of their counterparts in Europe and Australia. This is the unshakable conclusion that those who observe Islamic immigrant populations of their own countries reach. The last three years have borne witness to this fact: the Fort Hood shooting, the discovery of several prominent anti-American Muslim leaders in our midst, the strategic depositing of Sharia law as a matter of public debate, the accusations of persecution, and the demand for increased cultural sensitivity toward Muslim practices. The brazen push for an Islamic prayer center to be located on the site of the former World Trade Center, or in its close vicinity, is a flashing alert sign of the brightest color that the waters of American tolerance are being subjected to test and provocation.

Recognition of Sharia law in Western democracies is perhaps the most visible and pressing imperative for the Islamist. The Islamist wish is for everyone to be governed by Sharia Law, where there is little freedom and no compromise. Americans, the people with the greatest appreciation for the liberties of Western democracy, should recoil in horror at the strictures of Sharia law. Yet an unfathomable quest for recognition of these laws is sponsored by the secular elites who are unwilling to defend and secure Western civilization or the American republic. The Islamist, unlike the American, does not understand that human rights are embedded in the dignity of the human because the human is made in the image of God. Where America is about life, liberty, and the pursuit of happiness, Islam is about death, slavery, and the pursuit of power. It's the American dream and the Islamic nightmare.

The Muslim mind is inferior to the Christian mind because of Muslim ideas. Its ideas have not the virtue, the freedom, or the psychological fitness to compete with the Christian mind. The Islamist is the least innovative of men;

unproductive and regressive, his strength lies only in the creation of children and the vehemence of the spleen he vents toward the Westerner. The vast majority of humane and successful societies have had Judeo-Christian roots. Which Koran-based society has achieved this? Which Koran-based society offers liberty, human rights, tolerance, or openness? The fact is that the moral record of Islam is poor.

Americans must prepare themselves for probable full-scale war this century or the next with the Islamist. The objective outsider knows the demographics of Europe and the palsied and timorous nature of the European personality and politics, which has been exacerbated by the fallout of the Second World War. Because of changing demographics and a weakened Western world, a most substantial increase in Islamic power in this part of the world must be expected. In the likely war between the Islamist and America, certainly a day of infamy, Americans must eradicate the enemy as mercilessly and thoroughly as possible, as this is the attitude of the jihadist warrior. The more we bow, the more they will bomb. The more we relate, equate, and obfuscate, the weaker we become. The more we fear to offend and the more we hesitate to identify the enemy, the more they edge toward victory. Such a battle will bear the mentality of a street fight. The side that wants victory the most will win. The question is will America have the will? It will have to rely on its exceptional military tradition and its members that prefer death to capitulation. It must remember that this nation is the steward of liberty for the world.

It's time to limit radical Islam and jihad, not American freedom.

The Future

Many outsiders assert that the decline of America has begun. But this great nation is not timeworn; the eagle shows not even the slightest gray in some parts. The words of former president Reagan say it all: "Double—no, triple—our troubles and we'd still be better off than any other people on earth." *Damn straight.*

History suggests that the reign of America became formal with the conclusion of the Second World War, continued with the victory of the Cold War, and on into the twenty-first century. The events of the last century are indisputable facts since determining the real age of American hegemony is an imprecise science. Regardless, the terrorist attack on this soil in September 2001 awoke the nation, a sleeping giant roused from its slumber to find the battle lines drawn. And this is a battle the American is committed to. Retaliation and visible action must be seen from the United States in response to terrorism. Otherwise, the signal is that you can kill Americans with impunity. And that has disastrous consequences.

If socialistic views infest or dilute the values of the American people, the people will be susceptible, and worse, they will become victims of their enemies' agenda. A mountain of trouble may stand before this nation, but conservative Americans should know that history will be influenced by their actions. The following words are often attributed to the sixteenth president of the United States, Abraham Lincoln: "America will never be destroyed from the outside. If we falter and lose our freedoms, it will be because we destroyed ourselves." Such words ought to be etched in the minds of the citizens of this country, in both small towns and big cities. These words are staggeringly accurate.

The current enemies of the American people are unlike any in their history. Whereas in the past, enemies have been clearly identified, it is not true of the present or the future. They're harder to see and deal with. The biggest challenge facing America is ensuring its future is not the same as that of the great European civilizations of the past. That would be beyond tragic. But in addition to asking themselves, "Are we Rome?" Americans should ask themselves, "Are we England?" The decline and implosion of the once-mighty British Empire is one of the most depressing sagas of the twentieth century.

The American narrative is simultaneously compelling, unique, and rousing. This nation has met the precipice several times, teetering on the brink of disaster, loss, and mediocrity. Each time, it has recuperated with velocity and inaugurated a new era of exceptionalism and strength through fidelity to its values. A new battle was forged at the conclusion of the Second World War, seeking to fundamentally transform foundational ideas and values of Western society. These included patriotism and religion, and a push toward equality and relativism. It is a battle that until now America has sidestepped in large part. It was fortunate in that its transformation from the postwar era to Cold War America entrenched public opposition and fear of socialism. This has made it more difficult for the politically correct agenda to be implemented and elitist thinking to be accepted. Funny how God works. It was a positive side effect of the Cold War that it ingrained a fear of communism. It is arguably the one thing that kept America America.

American universities, while too frequently contaminated with proponents of socialism, remain not simply world-class but world-leading institutions, helping lead the way in science, business, and informatics. These universities are mostly flush with financial endowment, a situation unfamiliar to the educational institutions of the outsider's countries. This financial support allows greater emphasis on research and development. Americans must link, where possible, the college degree to the job, without impinging upon students' freedom or opportunity, to ensure their viability. Americans are exceptional in their work ethic and tend to have longer careers. In comparison, educated Europeans tend to remain in the workforce for less time, given the length of study at university or technical schools, and follow a mandated low retirement age.

Citizens of the developing world, from Lithuania to Poland to Eastern Europe to Africa, harbor great admiration for the American people and their way of life, and they seek to emulate the Americans. Even a silent, growing minority across Latin America and the Middle East shares these desires. Though this emerging trend is reported with near silence in the media, it should reaffirm America's values. Americans should celebrate these values, not apologize for them. Even more reason to be proud.

America must continue to be a refuge for the talented young of the outsider nations. Becoming an American is a notoriously difficult task. The green card may be the most elusive, and certainly the most exclusive immigration document in the world. Americans must make it easier for those who have great affection for freedom and who will enrich American society to gain their nationality. Importing educated talent in all areas must again become a priority for Americans. But Americans must be careful not to sully their mental image of immigration with the illegal variety that wreaks havoc on America's southwest borders. The media-academic complex has made the border a construct of bigotry—and it's not. A sovereign country will determine who comes to their country and the circumstances under which they come. Legal immigration always has and should continue to prolong and intensify American greatness.

The average American does not possibly grasp the nation's impact on human civilization and the wider world. The power Americans wield in their innovation, capitalism, and medical advances make them a staple in the cupboard of the outsider kitchen. Just as a candle cannot burn without fire, humanity cannot live without freedom, and it is America that provides the fire for the candle of freedom. Any free person, from wherever he or she may hail, is American.

The health of the world is delivered by both the figurative and literal medicine of the West, a civilization that has led with the model systems of law and politics. Americans, with their peerless international scientific advances, have assisted in scientific research. The consumer society and work ethic of the Industrial Revolution breathe life within the borders of this nation. But today the breathing is heavy and intermittent; many of the competitive edges of America and the West are blunted by the advances made in the rest of the world catching up, often by virtue of American trade and assistance.

Americans today find their civilization in peril: their problems financing public debt and the imbalance between their revenue and expenditure are the historical hallmarks of the decline of a superpower. *Debt is weight on your ankles.* The financial crisis has always featured in the collapse of civilizations, and this knowledge keeps Americans awake when they rest their heads on their pillows at night. They know they are encumbered by the worst crisis since the Great Depression, while Islam and secular Left ideology flourish. More anxious Americans even see parallels with the last occasion of the fall of the West: the once-great Roman Empire. Their understanding of tyranny has always been greatly more philosophical than that of other nations. Their sovereignty and civic pride steer them to the realization that tyranny affected through nanny statism is as detrimental to national morale as tyranny affected through violence.

This land would not be the first to succumb to the consequences of the "blessings of civilization" phase of its life, not the least of which is the loss of human liberty, the ultimate failure of success. This is, of course, hardly new, and many great thinkers have made such observations. But the American people cannot be usurped, unless they commit figurative suicide by losing confidence in their exceptional values, their faith, their abilities, and their history, thereby entering into the current status of other nations: stasis.

The success of Western civilization is not just in matters of science or technology or work ethic; those matters are only enabled through the Western principles that allow humanity to flourish and innovate. Americans must utilize their self-confidence to continually deliver the artisan product; they must take great care in their work and leave an impression of their own definitive style. They should never settle for second best; their infrastructure must symbolize their dominance. Remember, if you're not first, you're last.

A citizenry must believe in its nation state and must see themselves as such, not as world citizens, unless they have occasion to quell evil in other corners of the world in the pursuit of human freedom or to administer humanitarian aid. Americans subscribe to this more so than any other people, much to the chagrin of the outsider governed by leaders who hanker for a world devoid of any clear superpower. The internationalists. They would have America become just another seat at the dining table of world powers. There's only one thing worse than a socialist, and that's an international socialist.

The threat posed by internationalists, and their ideology is far greater than any nation-state overwhelming America and becoming the new global power. President Obama is a proponent of this threat, and this can be best seen in his approach to foreign policy.

It is fitting, then, that it is in the freedom-calloused hands of the American people that their own fate lies. Their quintessence of self-determination should always remain intact. If Americans are to continue, they must repel the nefarious and collectivist demands made of them by the outsider, demands generated by, at best, misjudgment, and at worst, envy.

The American people must be vigilant in ensuring that their government and its representatives reflect the intensely anti-socialistic, robustly individualistic, and deeply Christian nature of the nation. They must also avoid any form of cultural totalitarianism or Marxism, for it is these that inevitably lead to the mandatory conformity of conduct and thought. Tyranny over common sense and a subservience to political correctness should be smashed to smithereens. I didn't know God had appointed the Left as the arbiters of decency.

Where Americans find themselves right now, I believe, is not their permanent address, unless they allow it to be. In the life of every nation, no matter how inestimable their power or exceptional their people, exist hard seasons. But in these times, Americans must call upon their Christian decree, embedded in their makeup. If Americans believe God to be in control, directing their steps, then they must believe they are exactly where they are supposed to be. It is this strong faith that will carry Americans forward in their darkest hours and precisely this that sets them apart from any enemy, irrespective of magnitude or firepower. Faith turns spiritual pygmies into giants. Faith sees all problems as opportunity.

Americans have enormous reason for optimism. Their strengths have greater resonance in the world of today and of the future than ever before, equipping them to deal with the challenges of the new century. They must be aware that only the West, which they lead and have fashioned dramatically, can engender in the members of any polity, irrespective of size or location, the greatest potential for individual human creativity. Only those institutions—social, economic, and political—conceived by the Western bloodline ensure the best context for human achievement in the most challenging of circumstances.

Americans must recall the energetic flexibility and relentless optimism that have kept them ahead in the face of disruption and disappointment, and they must also remember their exceptional military tradition. They must remind themselves of the improbable experiment of their nation, of America's unique narrative: they are neither ordinary nor average. They should find solace in the words of the Texas Ranger: "No man in the wrong can stand up against a fellow that's in the right and keeps on a-comin'."[1]

Americans are a people in the right, with a resilience that sees them fall down seven times but get up eight. They must continue in this proud tradition and find an answer to every problem, not see a problem for every answer. The latter is the more common cause for the pessimist, mostly found in the socialistic nations. Faith is the essential ingredient of leadership.

As the SEAL finds comfort in the Bible's twenty-third psalm, so must the average citizen here. Hope must continue to grow deep in American bones, thriving in every inch. Americans must persistently see life as a leap of faith, a bold declaration of expectation. They must find meaning in life from the front line, not wait from the sideline for life to provide meaning. Americans do not find themselves; they create themselves. From the Navy SEAL to the New York firefighter to the Texas Ranger, each American has within an exceptional patriotism, a belief in Providence, a love of the military, a devotion to freedom, and a disposition to bravery. Going in for one more round when you don't think you can, makes all the difference.

America must not shrug its way to Belgium. It must stay the course; its people must remain devoted to the visions of its Founders and their documents, and must continue to be the bastion of optimism, freedom, individualism, and Christianity for the preservation of not just America, but humanity in total. Americans must retain their faith-based consciousness and must carry it with them in all the arenas of life. Cultural and national self-belief is the armor of a successful and confident America for the future. The secular nature of multiculturalism is at odds with the American society. In the same way as a human, America is not always right and is prone to error—I'm not saying it's perfect. Nor would I expect it to be, but the truth is, it's the best thing we have. Only the American people can secure Western civilization and the American republic. *May God be with them.*

The Nature of the American Boomerang

boomerang- n. a bent or curved piece of hard wood used as a missile by Aborigines, one form of which can be thrown so as to return to the thrower.

—The Macquarie Dictionary, Second Edition

This nation boasts an amazing number of individuals relentless in their pursuit and attainment of success, against all odds. Tocqueville once observed that "the greatness of America lies not in being more enlightened than any other nation, but rather in her ability to repair her faults."[1] Indeed, this has been America's legacy.

Americans possess a distinctly bold boomerang nature. Bearing the characteristics of the Australian flying tool, they often embark on a trajectory that takes them far from their origin but always returns them to their founding position. Both the boomerang and America are pioneer tools of self-determination, uniquely crafted in varying materials and size with an adventurous character and free will. Just like the American people, the boomerang leaves the hand of its thrower, and is exposed to dangerous temptation and external force, often momentarily accommodating it as it strays far from its anticipated course. But under the watchful eye of the eagle and God, and because of something intrinsic within their making, both always return.

Americans do have a difficult return journey, particularly because their trip back takes place in these hours of severely limited light. But as their past demonstrates, they have the capacity and the will, as well as the hand of God, on their side. Not even the finest boomerang can offer these qualities. Americans invariably return from an adverse journey better for it. *The damage is transient, not irreparable.*

This return journey must be traveled in the same space or vehicle that all other travel has occurred. It is often asserted in good faith by well-meaning, successful Americans that their nation would be well aided by orienting and realigning itself with the outside world, or that the answers to America's future lie in an entirely different approach. While it is true that America's famed formula must be updated and refreshed in order to meet the challenges of the future, it must not occur with global eyesight or a marked change in American politics or values. This is a time when Americans cannot afford to temper their values and reach a middle ground, deserting their passion. Instead, the return journey for Americans is always an authentic one, as noted in the famous words of one president: "There is nothing wrong with America that cannot be cured by what is right with America."[2]

Visitors to America's shores are powerfully inspired by what they witness, but they gravely fret over that which they have seen lost. They who consider themselves friends of America would implore its people to stand with the Founders of their nation in embracing and promoting the value of the individual and the exceptionalism of the American experiment. Americans must be jolted out of complacency. They must rise up with boldness, maintaining their dedication to the manifesto of freedom and patriotism. As I've said before, America wins respect in the world when it displays who it is and not what self-appointed cultural dietitians would want it to become.

As the American boomerang hurtles its way back to the promised land, friends of the Americans feel the need to remind them that freedom would have long ago shriveled and republican democracy waned in the other countries of the world were it not for them and their great country. For as long as this nation stands, this world will have a model of freedom and exception, a target to aim at, and a level to aspire to. Americans must not only remember but affirm their storied past. They must never forget who they are and where they came from. Truth be told, the silent majority of outsiders believe the future of world history is dependent on the future of this glorious nation. *America is the one Hall of Famer.*

Ronald Reagan, that great defender of American exceptionalism and global improvement, once said, "Freedom is never more than one generation away from extinction. We didn't pass it to our children in the bloodstream. It must be fought for, protected, and handed on for them to do the same, or one day we will spend our sunset years telling our children and our children's children what it was once like in the United States where men were free."

Americans must continue to see that individualism is the foundation of American society. They must also continue to instill in their young a distaste for submission to undue authority, and this must continue for the prosperity of this nation. *Never give up, and never have a master, save God.*

With the enemies lining up at the gates and with world sentiment convinced that the American experiment has finally expired, Americans must call on the official final words of the Navy SEAL:

> We train for war and fight to win. I stand ready to bring the full spectrum of combat power to bear in order to achieve my mission and the goals established by my country. The execution of my duties will be swift and violent when required yet guided by the very principles that I serve to defend.
>
> Brave men have fought and died building the proud tradition and feared reputation that I am bound to uphold. In the worst of conditions, the legacy of my teammates steadies my resolve and silently guides my every deed. I will not fail.[3]

Greatness is never awarded; it is always earned. Americans earn it with the fire and fight in their hearts—the quality that sets the extraordinary apart from the ordinary. All any individual of the slightest intellect can and must do is thank God for this nation and the true Americans that uphold her values.

Another simple but easily forgotten point: for America to continue to lead the world in freedom and hope, those conditions must continue to define the American existence at home.

One of the legs of my first speaking tour was spent in New York City. After delivering my speech at the Soldiers', Sailors', Marines', Coast Guard and Airmen's Club, a young lady sought me out. It turned out she was a volunteer for the Wounded Warrior Project, an organization dedicated to providing services and programs for severely injured servicemen and women. She said, "Your message must be heard by the New York firefighters. I work with them, and they will love you. You must come with me tomorrow, and I will take you around to as many firehouses as we can fit in." She knew the firefighters at various stations around the city because, in her volunteer work, she had organized them to sign and provide well wishes on cards for both current wounded warriors, many in Walter Reed Hospital, and for those still serving in Afghanistan and Iraq. I was given a personal tour of many fire stations all across New York, during which I met and spoke with dozens of New York's bravest, and spread my message. The fire stations are all patriotic and nostalgic venues, resplendent with American flags, and one really feels the heroism of the New York firefighter.

The firehouse that had the greatest impact was the FDNY Ten House, home of Ladder Company 10 and Engine Company 10, located on Liberty Street, directly across the road from where the World Trade Center once stood. It is the best-known firehouse in the world. I had the enormous honor of meeting firefighter and 9/11 hero John Morabito, a driver for Ladder 10, whose incredible story of survival has been the subject of much media attention. While he showed me around the firehouse, I heard his harrowing account of that day from morning to end, from the sound of those trapped in the World Trade Center who chose to jump, to being unable to drive due to the dead bodies lying on Liberty Street, to the loss of his six colleagues, to the complete annihilation of the firehouse, I felt sick. How could a city, a people, a nation ever recover from this? But they have. As President Bush said, "Here buildings fell, and here a nation rose."[4]

The story of Ladder 10 and John Morabito and the way this firehouse responded, not just on that day but in the years immediately after, is not only awe-inspiring and heartwarming; it exemplifies exactly why America is the incredible nation that it is today. The fifty-six-foot FDNY Memorial Wall on the side of the firehouse, as well as the Ten House Bravest 9/11 memorial inside, are testament to America's ability to remember and appreciate. Morabito told me that since that fateful day, people have asked him why he never sought professional therapy. His answer? "Nick, this is my therapy. Sitting on the front of this fire truck and talking to people every day, telling my story." Going into the future, America can be comforted that there are millions of John Morabitos. They can also rest well knowing that today's New York firefighter spirit represents what every American has bubbling inside: exceptional patriotism, a belief in Providence, a love of the military, a devotion to freedom, and a disposition to bravery.

A New Chapter:
How America Comes Back

I am on fire for liberty, prosperity, and a strong America, and I want more Americans to be committed to understanding what differentiates America from the rest of the world. I want to keep America number one.

It's a crucial time in American history. America is in the fight of its life. It is weaker today than it has ever been. The truth is that the Obama administration has been a spectacular failure. Nothing it has done has been aimed at keeping America number one. As a result, the world is a much more dangerous place.

Individualism, patriotism, and liberty—the unique properties of American life and culture—are at diminished levels. For the first time any of us can remember, America appears to be becoming irrelevant in world affairs.

But this is America. You can never count it out. It's time to embark on "Project America"—and to save America. The world needs an American renaissance. None of us want to even imagine a world where America is not running the show. Keeping America strong, saving it from a European future, is the great moral imperative of our time. There are many who want America down and never more to rise, but they should be ready to be surprised. America's elites must once more fall in love with what makes America different. This is still the country people cross oceans to get to. Still the place that sees people empty their life savings to be a part of. Still the nation for which people sell the shirts off their backs just to feel the American winds of freedom and opportunity. Still the country of the dreamer. If America were in as bad a shape as people have made out, there wouldn't be so many illegals sneaking across the border.

I want Americans to understand what is at stake for them and for people around the world if they choose to continue to drift from the virtues and values of traditional America. And I want them to realize what allowed them to become the greatest country in the world and stay there for so long—and what changed to bring them to where they are today.

I don't do this because I know America better than actual Americans. I don't. I couldn't possibly. But I believe I offer a unique perspective that may be helpful. Sometimes it takes someone on the outside to remind you what you are like. And I could be living in your future, and I'm here to tell you about it and what you can expect should you proceed with the fundamental transformation of America.

And I'll tell you what else I bring to the table: I offer truth. I introduce cold, factual reality to a discussion colored by envy and driven by the agendas of those who benefit from a weak America.

The media-academic corridor has a lot to answer for. It is an absolute disgrace to have professors parading as wardens, incarcerating the minds of the young, and watching the mainstream media carry the water for the Left. Intellectual integrity and moral courage must be returned to America's schools and newsrooms. That's why I make a point of speaking to as many high schools and colleges as possible. We must recapture our classrooms.

American exceptionalism is not an accident. Nor did it happen by chance.

It happened because America fostered a state that allowed its citizens the widest latitude for creativity and innovation. It rewarded success without government approvals and bureaucratic interference. It embraced religious faith, aspiration, and risk. And for those reasons, the people of America have been the most enterprising, market-oriented, individualistic, and averse to taxation and regulation to have ever walked the earth.

I do not believe for one second that America's best days are behind her. American decline is not inevitable. And those who say that America should manage its decline "gracefully" should be told rather indelicately what they can do with their opinion. Decline is a choice, not a condition.

Yes, America is falling behind, but only in fulfilling its potential. Take it from me: there is no other country in the world even close to America. The American model has offered, and continues to offer, a greater chance for dignity, hope, and happiness for more people than any other system of government has offered its own. If that weren't the case, you would not be dealing with the illegal immigration problem you currently have. You're wounded but not conquered.

You may not realize, but there are Americans all around the world doing great things for America. Doing so much to *keep* their country, to keep the improbable American experiment alive. In terms of values and a belief in American exceptionalism, middle America, or the center, still holds—it's the bottom and the top of the American polity that have changed the equation and endangered America's future. I've been blessed to have been able to travel the world in my twenty-nine years, and I am continually struck by some of these American works.

In December 2011 and January 2012, I spent an extended time in England and caught up with a friend from South Carolina who had come to study abroad at Oxford University through Summit Ministries. The Summit Oxford Study Centre is a study-abroad program combining the unique worldview approach of Summit Ministries with the academic strengths of Oxford, England. It fosters scholarship for church and culture, propelling Christian students forward as leaders in their disciplines and professions.

The program is run by profoundly exceptional Americans. They live just outside of Oxford, where there they educate young, academically successful students in a Christian and pro-American worldview. I had the remarkable privilege of sitting in on a couple of the sessions and getting to know the students and teacher, and was so deeply impressed by both the intellects and the patriotism evident, that words cannot accurately convey my sentiments. I distinctly recall thinking,

How many of these people are there out there? Scattered all over the world? And what other country is so forward thinking, so passionate about producing tomorrow's exceptional leaders, that it has programs running in foreign countries?

In June 2011, I was invited to give the keynote speech at the National 4-H Shooting Sports Invitational's closing ceremony in San Antonio, Texas. In front of me were more than a thousand coaches, competitors, and parents, representing almost every state in America. Across the nation, 4-H has more than six million members. And I had the opportunity to meet the teams of every state, pose for photographs, and be amazed by their courtesy, confidence, inquisitiveness, and how articulate they were. The thing I remember most was the pledge that was recited that night:

> I pledge my head to clearer thinking,
> my heart to greater loyalty,
> my hands to larger service, and
> my health to better living,
> for my club, my community, my country and my world.[1]

What a testimony to the American tradition. Just exceptional. To the bone. America may be in a lot of trouble, but it's important not to overlook its treasure. There are still tens of millions of Americans who are being faithful to the America we all know and love.

The current season in America is confusion. And it's time to think seriously, deeply, and searchingly. It's our job to inform: for an informed citizenry is the bulwark of democracy.

I believe there is a thirst for a mooring in America. And it has to be a belief in American exceptionalism. And the only people who can deliver it are patriotic forces with traditional values. The very values America appears to be walking away from are the ones that I believe the world should adopt.

How do we win this fight? How do we vanquish the forces that make us weak? How do we restore American glory? What does America have to do to come back?

Here's my fifteen-point plan for an American renaissance:

1. Exercise fidelity to the Constitution, Declaration of Independence, and founding ideals.

2. Promote and achieve a return to American self-belief as a force of nature. As any leader knows: you can't expect others to believe in you if you don't believe in yourself.

3. Reengage with cultural institutions. It is time for conservatives to compete for control of the cultural institutions that for the past four decades have been the forums and seedbeds of the Left. From Hollywood to popular music to teaching to journalism. The days of the cultural elites playing unopposed . . . they're numbered. We're coming to get you.

4. Put an end to the culture of complaint and entitlement. We need to put the professional offense-takers out of business. They're designed to intimidate us, to remove our confidence, to make us afraid to even look at someone the wrong way, to make all our visceral

convictions suspect. The days of promoting grievance and envy . . . they're over.

5. Stand up to bullies. America cannot allow itself to continue to be bullied by the anti-bullying crusade. It's time to punch the bully's nose.

6. Embrace rugged individualism. As I stated in chapter 3, rugged individualism is not an exercise in political nostalgia—it is a genuine solution for the myriad problems facing the United States in the twenty-first century. American national character must be understood in light of what it is: a self-made society. The world needs America to be a country of self-reliant warriors, not pussycats.

7. Recommit to success. If you ain't first, you're last. Work harder. Be the best. That's America. There is no virtue in striving for mediocrity. No American kid dreams of growing up to become the vice president. That's the way it has to stay.

8. Desire upward mobility. Upward mobility can never be replaced by downward stability. Taking a risk is virtuous.

9. Support Israel, always. Defend it to your last breath. It's a providential nation, and American success and purpose is linked to it. Supporting Israel is an American value.

10. Limit government. Nothing will extinguish liberty quicker than an activist government. Its goal is to turn adults into infants, and everyone into victims. There is nothing more obnoxious than a government whose

attitude is: "Don't worry; we know what is best for you." Limited government is an American thing. Keep it that way.

11. Ensure peace through strength. The uncommon valor America has shown against the sword of tyranny must continue. Weakness is provocative. Conviction is the mother of success. The United States military is the greatest vehicle against evil ever, and it's the noblest fighting force the world has ever seen. It must continue to be stronger than the rest of the world's militaries combined. America doesn't have to attend every argument it's invited to, but it does have a special role to play in the world as the guardian against chaos.

12. Smash political correctness. Political correctness empowers radical Islam, terror, and socialism. Advocates of the PC agenda are as dangerous to America as the men that orchestrated September 11. Margaret Thatcher said it best when she said "the world has never ceased to be dangerous, but the West has ceased to be vigilant."[2]

13. Restore character. While it may be substantially less vivid than in other places, there is a character problem in America that must be arrested. It was Dwight D. Eisenhower who said, "The spirit of man is more important than mere physical strength, and the spiritual fiber of a nation than its wealth." I urge Americans to understand and defend the sanctity of human life from conception until natural death. Anything less is evidence of a character deficit, and it weakens our "spiritual fiber."

14. Guard your Christianity closely. It is behind every-thing great about America—whether it's neighbor-liness, charitable works, or optimism. The more Christianity eroded in Europe, the poorer, less pow-erful, weaker, and less influential it became. John Adams wasn't joking when he said that the Constitu-tion was "designed for a religious and moral people" and was "wholly inadequate for any other."[3]

15. Remain economically massive and nimble. Capital and imagination must continue to combine more quickly in America than anywhere else in the world. Taxes must always be low, and government should be out of the way. Don't spend money you don't have.

That's my fifteen-point plan to reboot America and get it online again. That plan is the *real* "hope and change" America needs. Most important, there must be a consensus on what is wrong and right with America. Without it, America can never return to its full greatness. Consensus is not impossible, but its achievement will require patriotic Americans to assert themselves culturally and politically, and reenter the areas of education, media, and the arts.

I also believe America should be the energy arbiter of the world. Cars aren't the only thing that run on energy; world affairs do too. I consider the solution to many of this nation's—and the world's—problems to be under American feet. It must gain energy independence by exploiting its substantial oil and natural gas reserves. This will bring it economic prosperity, while weakening the influence of aggressive actors in the global theater. The pursuit of energy independence this way may not advance the liberal agenda, but green energy is both unaffordable and unnecessary. With the boom in recent times of shale oil, it appears this nation is on the right track. Americans should jump at a solution so easily within their literal grasp.

I consider it a national tragedy that America has seemingly abandoned space, a frontier it conquered. It is sad that this great chapter of American exceptionalism remains only as mere tourist attractions. It should be a matter of great concern to all Americans that America is unable to go into low-earth orbit, but other powers can. As with any departure America makes in any arena, a void will be filled by other powers, most likely less benign and desirable. America should never give any indication that it has stopped reaching for the stars.

To me, America is the hope that banishes hopelessness.

Our mission is clear. We need to rescue America. Through consistency, dedication, and faithfulness. Through going back to the beginning. By keeping the traditional family unit as your greatest treasure. By standing for liberty. By standing for the Constitution. By having a victory mentality, not a victim mentality. There must never be a closed sign hung on the final frontier.

We want an America where the weak become strong and the strong become great. Where you can still rise above the circumstances of your birth and achieve what you want to achieve. After freedom, inspiration is America's next greatest export. Anything is possible. Spread the word to your friends, neighbors, and acquaintances. And let what starts spread and spread across families, towns, counties, and states—let the steady trickle turn into a stream, and then a waterfall, and then an ocean. Let there be a patriotic flood that washes the pollutants and contaminants away.

America, your nation inspires me. You inspire me. You give me a reason to live. You're everything I thought you would be. It is my great privilege to serve you. I believe it's better to die on your feet than live on your knees. And I invite you to join me in this battle.

Help me help you, and let's preside over the strongest, proudest, and most prosperous America yet. We can do it. We must do. We will do it. What America needs most right now is strength, leadership, and will.

America must boomerang back.

ACKNOWLEDGMENTS

This book could not have been possible without the help of many.

I am grateful to the many Americans who hosted me during the time it took me to write this book. In particular, Randy and Maybeth Nunn, Eric and Becky Gerritson, Mark and Ann-Marie Murrell, Scott and Elizabeth McGuire, Steve and Susan Passariello, Noble and Cynthia Hathaway, Eddie and Mary-Ann Taylor, John and Sandra Parrott, Jamie and Jan Graham, Curtis and Suzanne Sanders, Ginni Thomas, Dianne Edmondson, John Rogitz, Nancy Theis, Justin Murff, Diane Fulton, Jack Temple, Dr. Mike Olcott, and Dave Goode.

I'm proud to call Col. Allen West my friend, and I'm honored he offered to write the foreword to this book. He inspires me every day.

The team at WND Books were magnificent, and I owe a great debt of gratitude to Joseph and Elizabeth Farah, Geoff Stone, and the entire marketing team.

I must thank my parents for their love and for constantly

sharpening me and expecting nothing less of me than excellence. Any success I have is theirs.

I thank Sanjay Gidwani for his unfailingly sound advice about everything from psychology to strategy, and for helping me rethink and revise my long-standing definition of *best friend*.

I wasn't blessed with brothers, but I got the next best thing in Evan and Angelo Angelopoulos. I thank them and their family, particularly Uncle George, for their love and support for as long as I can remember. From womb to the tomb, boys.

Others I must mention: Senator Ted Cruz, Governor Rick Perry, Attorney General Greg Abbott, Glenn Beck, Dr. Ed Feulner at the Heritage Foundation, Michael and James Mesiti, Nick and Peter Prilis, Jeremy Balkin, Kyle Kutasi, Ross Howes, Wes Selman, Alice Sullivan, Susan Fletcher, Lance Kennedy, Brendan Sharpe, Phil Meehan, Joanne Howarth, Jared Vallorani, Bill Whittle, Paul Rieger, Danny Diaz, Angelo Nunes, Jeffrey Field, Catherine Engelbrecht, Mickey Straub, Tom Qualtere, and Tim and Theresa Blake. I would also like to thank President George W. Bush. While I am yet to have the honor of meeting him, it was during his leadership that I truly began to love America, and wanted to start this journey. I consider him a very fine man; his refreshing moral clarity inspires me to this day.

To all the people who always believed in me—at school to university to over the years: thank you. Your loyalty will never be forgotten.

And to many, many more across the world who have extended me the warmest receptions and secured memories for a lifetime, you all make the sun shine.

Above all, I thank God for blessing me abundantly.

ABOUT THE AUTHOR

Nick Adams is an internationally renowned Australian speaker, lecturer, author, and media commentator. He is best known for his work in the field of American exceptionalism and is credited with a resurgence in the idea worldwide. He has spoken throughout America, Germany, South Korea, and the United Kingdom. He contributes to numerous media organizations and has received several state awards, including honorary citizenship, in America. Adams holds degrees in Media and Communications, Government and International Relations, Germanic Studies, and Education from the University of Sydney. In 2005, at the age of twenty-one, he was elected as the youngest deputy mayor in Australian history, a record he still holds to this day.

NOTES

INTRODUCTION

1. The White House, "News Conference by President Obama: Palaiz de la Musique et Des Congres, Strasbourg, France," news release, April 4, 2009, http://www. whitehouse.gov/the-press-office/news-conference-president-obama-4042009.

CHAPTER 1: THE COWBOY SPIRIT

1. Marcello Pera, introduction to *Christianity and the Crisis of Cultures*, by Joseph Ratzinger (San Francisco: Ignatius, 2006), 21.

CHAPTER 2: OLD GLORY

1. David Beckham with Tom Watt, *Beckham: Both Feet on the Ground: An Autobiography* (New York: HarperCollins, 2004), ix–x.
2. John Jay, "Federalist No. 2," in James Madison, Alexander Hamilton, and John Jay, *The Federalist Papers*, classic original ed. (n.p.: Tribeca, 2010), 3.

CHAPTER 3: FAITH

1. "Message from John Adams to the Officers of the First Brigade of the Third Division of the Militia of Massacusetts" (October 11, 1798), The Founding Faith Archive, at beliefnet, http://www.beliefnet.com/resourcelib/docs/115/ Message_from_John_Adams_to_the_Officers_of_the_First_Brigade_1.html, accessed January 9, 2014.
2. Dwight D. Eisenhower, in *America's God and Country: Encyclopedia of Quotations*, ed. William J. Federer (St. Louis: Amerisearch, 2000), 226.
3. Alexis de Tocqueville, *Democracy in America* (New York: Vintage, 1990), 93, 303–4.
4. Ibid., 308.

5. Ibid., 306.

6. Ibid., 305–6.

7. http://www.american.com/archive/2008/march-april-magazine-contents/a-nation-of-givers;
http://www.forbes.com/2008/12/24/america-philanthropy-income-oped-cx_ee_1226eaves.html;
http://www.philanthropyroundtable.org/topic/excellence_in_philanthropy/america_the_charitable.

8. James A. Reed, "The Later Life and Religious Sentiments of Abraham Lincoln," *Scribner's Monthly* 6, no. 3: July 1863, citing Noah Brooks, *Harper's Monthly*, July 1865, both quoted in *The Century Illustrated Monthly Magazine: Making of an American Project*, vol. 6, eds. Josiah Gilbert Holland and Richard Watson Gilder (n.p.: Scribner; Century, 1873), 340.

9. Quoted in Walter L. Hixson, *The Myth of American Diplomacy: National Identity and U.S. Foreign Policy* (Yale University Press, 2008), 37.

10. "U.S.-Israel Relations: Roots of the U.S.-Israel Relationship," WIS Virtual Library, http://www.jewishvirtuallibrary.org/jsource/US-Israel/roots_of_US-Israel.html; accessed January 2, 2014.

11. Tocqueville, *Democracy in America*.

CHAPTER 4: GOD'S TROOPS

1. Mark Divine, "SEAL Code: A Warrior Creed," NavySEALS.com, accessed January 6, 2014, http://navyseals.com/nsw/seal-code-warrior-creed/.

2. Douglas MacArthur, speech given at the US Military Academy (West Point, NY), May 12, 1962, quoted in Bernard K. Duffy and Ronald H. Carpenter, *Douglas MacArthur: Warrior as Wordsmith* (Westport, CT: Greenwood, 1997), 200.

CHAPTER 5: THE VALUE OF LIBERTY

1. Ronald Reagan, in a speech during a campaign rally for Vice President Bush, San Diego, California, November 7, 1988, http://www.quotationspage.com/quote/35947.html.

2. Margaret Thatcher, *Statecraft: Strategies for a Changing World* (New York: HarperCollins, 2002), xxv.

CHAPTER 6: COMPETITIVE CULTURE

1. The slogan of USA Network, a cable/satellite channel of American media and entertainment company NBCUniversal.

2. Alexis de Tocqueville, *Democracy in America: The Complete and Unabridged Volumes I and II*, trans. Henry Reeve (New York: Random House, 2004) vol. 2, bk. 1, chap. 8.

3. Henry Adams, *The Education of Henry Adams*, chap. 12 (1863). Available online at www.fullbooks.com.

CHAPTER 8: CONSTITUTIONALLY LIMITED GOVERNMENT

1. Paul A. Reahal, Proof (Maitland, FL: Xulon Press, 2004), 290, http://books.google.com.au/books?id=ZfyQ6_oiFFkC&pg=PA290&lpg=PA290&dq=%E2%80%9CThe+Bible+is+the+cornerstone+of+liberty+.+.+.+Students%E2%80%99+perusal+of+the+sacred+volume+will+make+us+better+citizens,+better+fathers,+and+better+husbands.%E2%80%9D&source=bl&ots=LuTm6MRgg4&sig=f0Wqd4eWiBwm4d0HtnfTGQQJgs8&hl=en&sa=X&ei=oNAgU7qpKomkkgWww4CQDg&ved=0CEEQ6AEwBA#v=onepage&q=%E2%80%9CThe%20Bible%20is%20the%20cornerstone%20of%20liberty%20.%20.%20.%20Students%E2%80%99%20perusal%20of%20the%20sacred%20volume%20will%20make%20us%20better%20citizens%2C%20better%20fathers%2C%20and%20better%20husbands.%E2%80%9D&f=false.

CHAPTER 9: TRADITION

1. Alexis de Tocqueville, *Democracy in America (Volume 2, Unabridged)*, trans. Henry Reeve (Stilwell, KS: Digireads, 2007), 31.
2. Marcus Luttrell, with Patrick Robinson, *Lone Survivor: The Eyewitness Account of Operation Redwing and the Lost Heroes of SEAL Team 10*, Google eBook (New York: Hachette Digital, 2007), prologue.
3. Alexis de Tocqueville, *Democracy in America: Part the Second, The Social Influence of Democracy*, trans. Henry Reeve, rev. Francis Bowen (New York: Langley, 1840; repr., New York: Knopf, 1945), 211.

CHAPTER 10: ARMED

1. *From the Wisdom of Our Fathers: Important Quotations to Instruct and Inspire* (blog at WordPress.com), http://founderswisdom.wordpress.com/category/cesare-beccaria/; accessed January 8, 2014.

CHAPTER 11: IMPERILED FUTURE

1. Quoted on the Socialism Quotes page of the website of the National Churchill Museum, http://www.nationalchurchillmuseum.org/socialism-quotes.html, accessed January 8, 2014.

CHAPTER 12: AN ALMOST TREASONOUS CULTURE WAR

1. Alexis de Tocqueville, *Democracy in America: A New Translation by Arthur Goldhammer* (Library of America, 2004) , 215.

CHAPTER 13: RADICAL ISLAM

1. Richard Kerbaj, "Muslim leader blames women for sex attacks," *The Australian*, October 26, 2006, http://www.theaustralian.com.au/news/nation/muslim-leader-blames-women-for-sex-attacks/story-e6frg6nf-1111112419114.

CHAPTER 14: THE FUTURE

1. Motto on the tombstone of Bill McDonald (Texas Ranger). See "Texas Ranger Hall of Fame (State Designated Memorial): William Jesse McDonald," on the website of the official Texas Ranger Hall of Fame Museum, http://www.texas-ranger.org/halloffame/McDonald_Jesse.htm.

CHAPTER 15: THE NATURE OF THE AMERICAN BOOMERANG

1. Alexis de Tocqueville, *Democracy in America*, Volume II (1840), available online at www.columbia.edu/cu/tat/core/tocqueville.htm.
2. Bill Clinton, inaugural address, archived at CBC Digital Archives, at http://www.cbc.ca/archives/categories/politics/international-politics/swearing-in-us-presidential-inaugurations/bill-clintons-first-day.html.
3. Mark Divine, "SEAL Code: A Warrior Creed," NavySEALS.com, accessed January 6, 2014, http://navyseals.com/nsw/seal-code-warrior-creed/.
4. "Text: President Bush's Acceptance Speech to the Republican National Convention," *Washington Post*, Politics, September 2, 2004, http://www.washingtonpost.com/wp-dyn/articles/A57466-2004Sep2.html.

CHAPTER 16: A NEW CHAPTER: HOW AMERICA COMES BACK

1. The 4-H Motto, from the page titled "4-H Motto, Creed and Pledge," on the website of the National 4-H History Preservation Program, http://4-hhistory-preservation.com/History/M-C-P/, accessed January 9, 2014.
2. Margaret Thatcher, *Statecraft: Strategies for a Changing World* (New York: HarperCollins, 2002), xxv.
3. "Message from John Adams to the Officers of the First Brigade."

INDEX